24

LONG ROADS HOME

Tim Griffiths

Tim Griffiths

Published in 2024 by FeedARead.com Publishing

Copyright © The author as named on the book cover.

First Edition

The author has asserted their moral right under the Copyright, Designs and Patents Act, 1988, to be identified as the author of this work.

All Rights reserved. No part of this publication may be reproduced, copied, stored in a retrieval system, or transmitted, in any form or by any means, without the prior written consent of the copyright holder, nor be otherwise circulated in any form of binding or cover other thanthat in which it is published and without a similar conditionbeing imposed on the subsequent purchaser.

A CIP catalogue record for this title is available from the British Library.

TABLE OF CONTENTS

For those who come after

We are, or should be at the very least, at war with the forgetting. Maybe it is a fight we cannot win, but still it matters to fight the darkness. The warning of *Y Gododdin* is that all shall be forgotten.

Neil Oliver, *Wisdom of the Ancients*

I want us to be doing things, prolonging life's duties as much as we can. I want Death to find me planting my cabbages, neither worrying about it or the unfinished gardening.

Montaigne, *Essays*

Other books by Tim Griffiths

A Place Quite Northward — FeedARead 2015

North of England and Scotland in 1704 — FeedARead 2018

The Sanctuary Records of Durham and Beverley — Durham County LHS 2022

CHAPTER 1

A CHINESE WEDDING

The date: Saturday 13th October 1934.
The scene: the chapel of the British Embassy in Peking, then known as Peiping.
The occasion: the marriage of Owen Ambrose Griffiths and Marjorie Mary Vicker.

On 14th October the Official Newsletter of the British Embassy contained the following report:

> A very representative company assembled yesterday morning at the British Legation Chapel for the marriage of the popular chaplain of the British Legation, the Rev O A Griffiths, to Miss M M Vicker, who had lately arrived in Peiping from England. The chancel was decorated with palms and white chrysanthemums. Members of the corporals' mess of the British Legation Guards acted as ushers. Dr W H G Aspland gave away the bride, Mrs H H Molland was matron of honour and Mr John Reeves, student-interpreter of the British Legation, best man. Dr S K Chang of the PUMC [Peking Union Medical College] presided at the organ. The Right Rev F L Norris, Bishop in North China, made a feeling and appropriate address to the newly married pair.

The wedding was followed by a reception in the Ambassador's residence, where Dr Aspland, whom we shall meet later as the pathologist in the case of Pamela Werner, made a 'most felicitous' speech as best man, a speech which included a very Chinese toast to the bride and groom – 'long life, good luck and every happiness'. Among the guests were Dr G A M Hall of the Peking Union Medical College and Mrs Timothy Lin, wife of the principal of the Ch'ung Tê School. Both these organisations would be significant in the story of Owen and Marjorie's life in China. After tiffin at Dr Aspland's the bride and groom left for their honeymoon in the Western Hills outside the city. On the return the newly married couple would live at the Ch'ung Tê School, Jung Hsien Hutung, West City.

Although there are Chinese ingredients on the margin of this report the mention of 'tiffin' points to the quintessentially British style of expatriate life in the age of empire and colonialism. Despite Owen's original intentions to undertake missionary work the shared life of Marjorie and himself for the next few years would take place mainly within the sheltered walls of the Legation Quarter, a European fortress and haven in a potentially hostile land. That the British Embassy remained in Peking, despite the fact that the Chinese government was then situated in Nanking, was an echo of earlier imperial struggles between China and Western powers. The Boxer rebellion in 1900, during which many missionaries and other foreign nationals had been killed, had terminated with a lengthy siege of the earlier Legation area and after the siege the Western powers had insisted on creating a fortified enclave in central Peking which they were not prepared to abandon to move to more exposed buildings in Nanking.

It is difficult nowadays to find the Bishop's sermon, reprinted in full in the newsletter, either feeling or appropriate. It contains wise words, reminding Owen and Marjorie that the task of becoming 'one flesh' is an ideal set before them, an ideal to be achieved only with much difficulty and self-sacrifice. But one may suspect that this was the Bishop's standard marriage sermon, brought out and dusted down for each newly married couple. It contains absolutely nothing of personal relevance to the lives of Owen and Marjorie, or to the strange journeys that each of them had made in the years before their marriage.

Something of this strangeness may be glimpsed in the wedding photos, in which the couple appear posed and formal, perhaps rather tense. Marjorie Vicker, 'lately arrived in Peiping', had embarked on 4th September on the P&O ship SS Rajputana bound for Yokohama with 104 passengers. Described on the passenger list as a 'missionary' she had travelled second class from London to Shanghai on a voyage lasting at least five weeks. Intermediate ports of call were Marseille, Port Said, Aden, Colombo, Penang, Singapore and Hong Kong. but on any reckoning Marjorie seems unlikely to have arrived in Shanghai much before 9th or 10th October. Owen had travelled down to Shanghai to meet her when she disembarked. That in itself was quite a journey. Two years later the American traveller Graham Peck travelled the same route in the opposite direction. His train left Peking in the late afternoon and, after stopping at Tientsin on the east coast, made its slow way south to the Yellow River and eventually to the north bank of the Yangtze at Nanking, arriving there about 30 hours after leaving Peking. The whole train was then transported across the river on a barge before continuing its journey through a second night towards Shanghai, arriving there on the following morning. The ferry crossing of the Yangtze continued to operate for another 34 years until the massive road & rail bridge was opened in 1968. While Peck's journey took less than 48 hours others were not so fortunate. China was in the grip of fighting between rival warlords, and the train could be delayed because of the fighting. At times soldiers rode shotgun to protect the train from attack by bandits.

On their journey north Owen and Marjorie may have spent a night in the British Legation at Nanking before rejoining the train and taking the ferry over the Yangtze to travel north to Peking. By the time of their arrival at the station in Peking, quite possibly on the day preceding their wedding, they must both have been shattered, and it is hardly surprising that the highly intelligent Marjorie entered her age incorrectly on the marriage certificate.

Having been in China since March of the previous year Owen would at least have had friends and acquaintances among the guests assembled in the chapel and at the wedding-breakfast. Marjorie would have known no one, not even her matron of honour. This sudden introduction to a totally foreign country and to the life of the Legations in Peking probably made her feel, like Dorothea Casaubon in *Middlemarch*, that she was 'tumbled out among incongruities'. The next six years were however to prove the happiest of her life.

The main part of this book will cover the period from Owen's arrival in China in early 1933 to his final return to England in 1945 after four years of separation during the War. I will cover more briefly their life in England after the War, but we must start by telling the family history that lies behind this most improbable marriage.

CHAPTER 2

OUR ANCESTORS

Owen's Paternal Ancestry – The Agricultural Heritage

While Owen was the son of an agricultural labourer his family history offers a picture more varied than we might have expected. His great great grandmother Mary Griffiths (1773-1864) was born in Sandhurst outside Gloucester and lived there throughout her life. Married with 4 sons she became a widow but continued to farm an 18 acre smallholding with the help of her family and of 2 employed labourers. William, her second son born in 1801, also farmed in Sandhurst and was described as a yeoman farmer, an indication that he considered himself as having a certain social status in the community. After losing his wife he moved back in with his mother until her death in 1864. Mary's death was reported in the Gloucester Journal for Saturday 21st May 1864: "May 16, at Sandhurst, in the 91st year of her age, Mrs Mary Griffiths, an old and respected inhabitant of that place". Mary had remained in occupation of the farm up to the time of her death and on 19th September of that year the live and dead farming stock was auctioned, together with the dairy utensils, farm implements, hay, straw, and fruit and potatoes awaiting harvest. The date of the auction reflects the need to clear the farm before the new tenant took possession on 23rd September, the customary quarter day. Although Mary Griffiths probably did not own a freehold interest in the farm she did have such an interest in 3 adjoining cottages which were sold at auction on 5th May 1865, subject to the existing tenancies. Also sold at that auction was a piece of good meadow land measuring just under an acre and a plot of garden land measuring just over 1¼ acres. This second plot was sold "together with the Allotment to be made in respect of the same under the Sandhurst, Norton, and Wotton Inclosure, now in progress". The relevant local Inclosure Act became law in 1865 and the allotments referred to in the auction particulars were made in 1867. The new owner of the 1¼ acre plot would have lost this plot as a result of the inclosure but would have received one or more different plots in compensation.

The auction particulars indicate that Mary Griffiths was not only "an old and respected inhabitant" but also a prosperous smallholder with a small dairy herd and land available for arable crops, fruit and vegetables. It is perhaps surprising that as a tenant farmer she also held the freehold interest in 3 cottages and 2 plots of agricultural land.

> Despite this apparent prosperity Owen's ancestors were never free of the shadow of the workhouse. Mary had a granddaughter, Fanny Griffiths, born in 1839 and living with her at the time of the 1851 census. 10 years later Fanny is recorded as an inmate of the Gloucester Union Workhouse, being described as "blind 2 years" and "idiotic".

After Mary's death William moved in with his eldest brother Joseph (c.1795-1878) who would become Owen's great grandfather. Joseph was the only son not to stay in Sandhurst. He moved to Hucclecote where he worked as an agricultural labourer, a somewhat surprising choice for a man whose mother and younger brother were both successful farmers. His wife Mary, also born around 1795 in Hucclecote or Churchdown, had to work to supplement the family income In 1841 therefore Joseph was living in Hucclecote with the 4 children of their marriage while Mary was a live-in female servant at a villa in Churchdown. 10 years later the couple were back together but even in her seventies Mary was earning money as a female dressmaker. By this time Joseph had switched from being a labourer to being a dealer, presumably in cattle, and he also appears to have benefited from the sale of his mother's farm property since by the end of the 1860s he had moved to Butts Cottage in Brockworth. This was almost certainly a property which he owned since the Gloucestershire Chronicle for 12th June 1880 gives notice of an auction to be held on the following Friday at the Hare and Hounds Inn in Churchdown, one of the lots being "At Brockworth - A Cottage and Garden, adjoining the Turnpike Road leading from Gloucester to Cirencester, to which it has an extensive frontage, late in the occupation of Joseph Griffiths, deceased". A cottage at the Butts in Brockworth, which may be same property then in the ownership of the Colwell family, was requisitioned in 1921 as part of the land required for Brockworth aerodrome. This would have formed part of the land subsequently occupied by the Gloucester Aircraft factory, famous for the work of Frank Whittle on the development of the jet engine.

Joseph suffered senile decay and died at the age of 82 or 83 on 27th August 1878. His wife Mary probably died in the same decade as she does not appear in the 1881 census. It was their second child and eldest son John Henry (c.1825-1901), almost always referred to simply as Henry, who became Owen's grandfather. Henry was born in 1825 or 1826. After a childhood spent at home he followed his father's example and moved out in search of work as an agricultural labourer. In 1851 he was employed as a farm servant by William and Mary Hopton in Ashchurch just outside Tewkesbury. He married Hannah Jones in Bredon on 9th September 1858 and they started their married life in a small property in Evan's Alley off Barton Street in Tewkesbury.

Hannah Jones (1833-1901), like her new husband, came from a local agricultural background. Born in 1833 in Eldersfield as the third child and eldest daughter of Joseph and Ann Jones she was baptised there on 13th October and grew up at Nursery Cottage. Her father Joseph, an agricultural labourer, had been born around 1806 and had married Ann Morgan in Eldersfield on 14th January 1828. The couple had at least 8 children: John, Joseph, Hannah, Marie, James, Sarah, Caroline, and Eliza. By 1851 all except the youngest were out at work.

John (1830) and James (1837) were living at home but working as agricultural labourers, presumably on a nearby farm.
Joseph (1831) was a lodger with William Jenkins (a carrier) and his wife Elizabeth at their home in Pendock between Gloucester and Ledbury. He was also working as an agricultural labourer.
Hannah (1833), shown in the record as Anna Jones, was a house servant with Thomas and Grace Barnett at Rushmoor Hill Farm in Bredon.
Maria (1835) was also a servant, with Thomas and Elizabeth Hartland at a farm in Forthampton near Tewkesbury.
Sarah (1839) is shown as a visitor with William and Mary Stallard in Bredon. At the age of 12 she was working in a silk mill.
Caroline (1841), shown on the record as aged 9, was a servant with Thomas and Mary Jenning at Little Dunshill Farm in Eldersfield.

This was an age of child labour, an unavoidable necessity for parents with insufficient income to support a large family and without any access to social security.

By 1861 Joseph and Ann Jones had moved to Bredon. Their daughter Eliza was still living at home but now working as a glover, and a granddaughter Ann was also living with them, probably on a visit from Manchester where she was born. Joseph's wife Ann may have died before 1871 as she is not shown in the census for that year. Joseph was then living at Blakes Cottage in Bredon together with Eliza and her husband Joseph Humphries and their baby Ernest. Joseph Humphries was born in Gloucestershire and also worked as an agricultural labourer. Another of Joseph Jones's granddaughters, Catherine aged 3, is also recorded.

As noted above Henry and Hannah Griffiths started their married life in Evan's Alley off Barton Street in Tewkesbury. This accommodation would have been cramped and noisy. There were 9 cottages in the alley, as well as the shop of Mr Evans the nail maker. While they may have had other children who died in infancy their two surviving children were Emily Rosa, born in 1864, and William Henry, born on 16th December 1866 and later to become Owen's father.

> The life of Owen's aunt Emily Rosa is rather a puzzle. She was still living with her parents in 1891 and 1901 with no declared occupation or other source of income. After their death in 1901 she moved to a property in the Longdon Heath area of Upton where the 1911 census shows her as living on private means. She died in the late summer or autumn of 1918, aged 53 or 54. Her private means may have been no more than required for a frugal existence but it is nonetheless surprising that a spinster from this family did not have to work for her living.

Henry and Hannah lived in Evan's Alley for about 20 years before moving to Monsel Lane in Upton on Severn, a village then as now subject to periodic flooding from the river. They remained there for the rest of their lives, both dying within a few weeks of each other in 1901. Henry died on 3rd September from senile decay and paralysis and Hannah on 28th October from heart disease and general dropsy.

Hannah's death was recorded in the Worcestershire Chronicle on 9th November.

An unusual feature of the census returns for Henry and Hannah is the number of boarders and visitors recorded. In 1861 the 3 month old Henry William Davis is shown as a boarder. The most likely explanation is that Hannah, having lost a child of her own, was employed as a wet nurse. A child with this name is recorded as being born on 28th December 1860, the parents being David and Mary Davis of Cowfield Farm in Ashchurch. Mary's maiden name was Hopton and at the time of the census they were visiting her parents at the farm where Henry Griffiths was employed as a labourer. In 1881 Sidney Jones and Edith Humphries, both under 2 years old, are shown as visitors. They are probably family members, in all likelihood a nephew and niece of Hannah, Edith being the daughter of Joseph Humphries and his wife Eliza, who was Hannah's youngest sister. The 1901 census shows 2 boarders, Fanny Vine (aged 6) and Kate Vine (aged 4) both born in Upton. The school admission records for Fanny in 1898 and 1900 shows her address as the Union Workhouse in Upton (originally founded in 1835). The record for 1900 gives her birth date as 5th May 1894 and shows her parent's name as Hannah. This suggests either that Hannah was a young widow or that she was an unmarried mother. The census list for the workhouse in 1901 does not include anyone with the name of either Hannah or Vine. It is unclear how Fanny and Kate came to live as boarders with John Henry and Hannah, but it is possible that Henry and Hannah received some payment from the workhouse to take care of the children.

Henry and Hannah's only surviving son William Henry (1866-1941) was to be Owen's father. Born on 16th December 1866 he spent his childhood years in Tewkesbury and Upton before taking work as a porter at the Foley Arms Hotel, an old coaching inn in Great Malvern. He was one of twelve employees of this well known establishment. At the time of the 1891 census there were four visitors: two single ladies of independent means, and a married couple called John and Edith Reid. Edith Reid had been born in Scotland and her husband John was probably also Scottish though born in Bengal. It is likely that they employed the 3 servants also staying at the hotel: a lady's maid, a coachman, and a footman.

William Henry married Annie Phoebe Edwards on 9th October 1895 and they moved into Conway Cottage in Cemetery Road, Great Malvern. They had however clearly slept together before their marriage as their first son Victor William was born at the cottage on 21st March, five and a half months after the wedding.

Owen's Maternal Ancestry – London Trades

Owen's mother Annie Phoebe Edwards (1866-1944) was the eldest of 8 children born to Thomas Henry Edwards and his wife Sarah Ann Merry. Thomas Henry was a journeyman cabinet maker working in St Pancras so that Owen's maternal family had their immediate roots in subsistence level London trades rather than in agriculture.

However Annie Phoebe's maternal grandparents, Richard Hunt Merry (c.1806-1856) and Sarah Jorns (c.1806-?1856) both came from the small village of Clifton south of Banbury in Oxfordshire. Both born around 1806 they were living in London as a married couple by June 1844 when their elder daughter Sarah Ann Merry was born at 61 Brunswick Street in Southwark. The registration district for her birth was Saint Saviours Union, the Southwark workhouse, but it is unclear whether this means that her parents were then or had previously been inmates of that institution. Richard Merry was in work as a porter or carman, responsible for using a horse and cart to deliver gin from one of the many London distilleries. By 1849, when their second daughter Emma was born, they had moved to Bethnal Green and then moved again shortly afterwards to Alfred Place in Cripplegate.

By 1851 Richard and Sarah were living in Alfred Place in Cripplegate with Richard still working as a carman. Richard died on 10th May 1856 in St Bartholomew's Hospital and received a non-conformist burial in the Victoria Park Cemetery in Hackney. The cause of death is recorded as erysipelas, a streptococcal skin disease which often proved fatal before the discovery of antibiotics. Since this disease is also highly infections it is possible that Sarah died at much the same time although I have not been able to trace her death certificate. By the date of the census in 1861 their two children were orphans, and the younger daughter Emma was living as a visitor with William and Ann Lymath in Great York Mews, Marylebone. William Lymath, born in 1806 in Great Tew, came from a family of blacksmiths and had worked as a shoeing smith in Oxfordshire until the end of 1838 when his partnership with William Gibbons had been dissolved by mutual consent. His wife Ann was born in Deddington, the village immediately next to Clifton. It is probable that William and Ann were childhood friends of Richard and Sarah Merry and therefore willing to look after their orphaned children until they were old enough to make their own way in the world. In Emma's case she probably entered domestic service until her marriage in March 1871 to an upholsterer Frederick Swain.

As noted above Sarah Ann Merry (1844-1929). Owen's grandmother, was born in Southwark but spent part of her childhood in Bethnal Green where her sister was born. Faced like her sister Emma with the likely choice between domestic service and prostitution she may be the 18 year old servant listed in the 1861 census as Sarah Moore living with Abraham and Elizabeth Jessup in Lewisham. Her birthplace is shown as Bethnal Green, the area where she lived as a child. We can be more confident about her next appearance in the records which evidences her marriage in Marylebone to Thomas Henry Edwards on 7th December 1865 when, in the absence of her parents, her sister Emma acted as witness.

Sarah Ann's husband was Thomas Henry Edwards (1840-1913), a journeyman chair-maker born in St Pancras in June 1840 and still living and working in that part of London. We had better call him Thomas Henry Junior since his father was also named Thomas Henry Edwards (c.1814-1889) and worked in the same trade as a chair-maker. Thomas Henry Senior had been born in Bath around 1814 and as a young man had come in search of work to London where he met and married Phoebe Langley (1815-1891) in St Pancras on 30th April 1837. Phoebe was a couple of years younger than her husband and had been born in Oxford where she was baptised on 22nd January 1815 in All Saints Church. Her parents are recorded as Joseph and Phebe (sic) Langley living in Amsterdam in this parish, and Joseph is shown as being a carver and gilder. The building then known as Amsterdam is now known as Jeune Hall in Jeune Street in the area to the east of the city over Magdalen Bridge[1]. As Phoebe gives her birth place as Oxford Market it is possible that her father Joseph may have had a stall there. She had probably come to London as part of a family group as in 1841 she was living in Carey Street, St Clement Danes off the Strand with her husband Thomas, their eldest child Thomas, and three members of Phoebe's family: Joseph (age 30) and Thomas (age 20), presumably her brothers, and Phoeby (sic), aged 60 who was probably her mother. Since Thomas is recorded as having been born in Middlesex in 1821 it is possible that the family had moved to London when Phoebe was a young child. It would of course have been quite reasonable for her father to seek better trading opportunities in London.

Thomas Henry Edwards senior spent his working life as a jobbing cabinet maker in St Pancras. At some point they moved to Charles Street where their daughter Louisa was born in 1853, and then to 25 Warren Street which was their home for about 20 or 25 years. In their old age Thomas Henry and Phoebe moved into the St Pancras Almshouses, 'an asylum for decayed and deserving ratepayers of the parish'. It is good to know that they were deserving, even if decayed, although the adjective reflects the enduring Victorian debate (still alive today) on the distinction between the deserving and undeserving poor. Thomas Henry died in 1889 and Phoebe in 1891, both being shown as 75 years old at the time of death. Thomas Henry suffered from chronic bronchitis and heart problems while the causes of Phoebe's death are recorded as cerebral disease and coma.

Thomas Henry Edwards Junior was born in St Pancras and baptised at Old St Pancras on 21st June 1840. There are no details of his early life but by the age of 20 he was working as a chair-maker in his father's business and still living with his parents. On 19th July 1862 he married Jane Mary Holmes and their son Henry Thomas was born on 26th December 1863. However Jane Mary then died on 31st January, just 5 weeks after the birth. The cause of death was

---

[1] I am grateful to Pauline Mills for identifying Amsterdam in Oxford.

given as phthisis, an old term for consumption or tuberculosis. Victorian doctors were aware that the symptoms of this disease were often masked during pregnancy but that women were at high risk of death in the period immediately following childbirth. Thomas Henry thus became a widower at the age of 23. Henry Thomas, the child of this first marriage, was probably taken care of by his paternal grandparents and was living with them at the time of the 1871 census. He may be the person of that name who died in London in 1945 at the age of 81.

When Thomas Henry married Sarah Ann Merry on 7th December 1865 this was therefore his second marriage, but this marriage would last for over 47 years until his death in 1913. Thomas and Sarah had 8 children, all of whom survived into adulthood, a remarkable record for a poor family living in the unhealthy streets of nineteenth century London. Their eldest child was Annie Phoebe who married William Henry Griffiths in 1895 and became Owen's mother.

With Thomas Henry Junior we make our final visit to the world of the workhouse for by 1911 Thomas Henry had moved to the St Pancras Auxiliary Workhouse at St Anne's Home, Streatham Hill. This building was used by the St Pancras trustees from 1890 to 1915 to accommodate about 500 aged and infirm males. Conditions in the workhouse were undoubtedly grim, with residents sleeping in vast barrack-like dormitories, eating a poor and monotonous diet, and with little to entertain them during the long days. His final years cannot have been as comfortable as those of his parents, living together in the much more homely almshouses. We do not know why he moved there. He may well have suffered from senile dementia or from some physical condition that made it impossible for him to be cared for at home. Still an inmate, he died of heart failure on 16th February 1913. When Thomas Henry moved to the workhouse, where of course Sarah could not live with him, she moved in with her son James Edwin, a coach smith in Camden Town. She lived on until 1929 when, at the age of 85, she also succumbed to heart failure at the Hammersmith Infirmary, located in Ducane Road next to the Hammersmith workhouse and to Wormwood Scrubs Prison.

Owen's Parents

We do not know when or how Owen's parents first met. As noted above William Henry was working as a waiter in Great Malvern in 1891. Annie Phoebe had probably moved to Worcestershire around 1890, where she had found work as a cook in Bredon, just outside Tewkesbury. Her employers were Hugh Houston, a retired army Major, and his wife. Local directories show that the major was a long-established resident of Bredon. He may also have had property in London, or have belonged to a club there. Possibly he engaged Annie as his cook during one of his visits to the capital. As the eldest daughter of a large family Annie would have gained much useful experience in cooking and domestic management whilst her mother was nursing one child or expecting the next. The youngest daughter, Florence, was born in 1884, by which time Annie was nearly 18 years old.

We do not know what Annie was doing between 1891 and her marriage on 9th October 1895. She may not have remained in the employment of Major and Mrs Houstown as she gave her address at the date of marriage as the small hamlet of Earl's Croome, just outside Upton on Severn. Possibly she was by then working for another family. Great Malvern is some miles from Earl's Croome, but it may have been where she shopped on behalf of her employer or spent her days off. It is likely that she visited William Henry's rooms in Malvern, since their first child Victor was born on 21st March 1896, five and a half months after their marriage. They started their married life together at Conway Cottage, Cemetery Road, Great Malvern. By the time of the wedding William Henry had already left his job at The Foley Arms to become a journeyman painter. Possibly marriage, or premarital sex, was considered incompatible with a job at the hotel. It would certainly have put a stop to Annie's employment as the domestic servant of a respectable family. None of Annie's family acted as witnesses of the marriage, and quite probably none were present. We simply do not know if Annie ever saw her parents or her seven brothers and sisters after her move to Worcestershire. On both her side and theirs the cost of travelling between her new home and London may have been prohibitive.

Within a couple of years of their marriage William Henry and Annie moved from Great Malvern to Holdfast, where their second son Archibald was born on 22nd December 1897. From there they moved to The Old House in Queenhill where Owen was born on 23rd October 1901 and his younger sister Eva in 1905. According to the 1911 census there were 5 children of the marriage, of whom one had died by that date[2]. The Old House still stands. Now a single dwelling it was previously divided into 3 separate units. By this time, and probably by the time of their earlier move to Holdfast, William Henry had taken employment as an estate painter and journeyman worker on the Pull Court Estate owned by the wealthy Dowdeswell family. Certainly by 1921 they had moved into Pull Court Cottages on the estate, with William now described as a general painter in the employment of Rev G B Dowdeswell. Annie was now in service as the housekeeper in Pull Court where Eva was also employed as a housemaid. The only family member not employed at Pull Court was Archibald who worked elsewhere as a carpenter. The 1921 census also records Ellen Bushell, a 26 year old servant working as a parlour maid for Rev G B Dowdeswell and no doubt paying rent for board and lodging with William and Annie. William would remain working on the estate until his retirement and the 1939 register shows him, Annie and Archibald living at The Lodge, Bushley, a retirement cottage on the estate. Archibald is now described as an aircraft inspector and no doubt had much work to do over the following 6 years. William died of a cerebral haemorrhage on 22nd August 1941. His funeral was the subject of a brief article in the Tewkesbury Register of 30th August which records that he died at the age of 74 after being employed at Pull Court for very many years. The mourners were his widow, their 2 older sons Victor and Archie, their daughter Eva with her husband, and a sister-in-law named as Mrs T Lane (presumably one of Annie's sisters with her husband's initial). Neither Owen nor Marjorie were able to be present as Owen was still in Peking while Marjorie had recently moved to Vancouver.. Annie Phoebe survived her husband by a little more than 2 years, dying of cerebral thrombosis at Mitton, Bredon on 6th January 1944 during Owen's years of internment in the Philippines. Her death certificate shows her final address as Mitton, Bredon while a brief note in the Gloucestershire Echo dated 7th

[2] Beatrice Eva, born in late 1899 and died on 1 February 1900 at the age of 6 weeks (information supplied by Trisha Paterson). William and Annie were already living at Queenhill at the date of Beatrice's death.

January states that she died at Merden Cottage, Bredon Road, Tewkesbury, the residence of her daughter Eva Sweet. Additionally her death certificate records her occupation at Croft Farm, Bredon's Hardwick. The 1939 register shows that Eva Sweet and her husband Bartholomew were then living at Verdon Cottage in Bredon's Hardwick, adjacent to Mitton Cottage in the same hamlet. It is therefore likely that after William's death Annie moved to live next to her daughter and may have supplemented a meagre pension with some domestic service at the nearby farm (which I have not traced in the records).

It is very probable that Owen knew none of his grandparents. His father's parents Herny and Hannah both died in the year of his birth, while his mother's parents Thomas Henry and Sarah lived far away in London and were probably too poor to contemplate the cost of a visit to Queenhill. The theme of poverty, or living on the breadline, is common to the different strands of Owen's family. Whether agricultural labourers or journeyman workers they all lived from hand to mouth, with the workhouse as a potential retirement home, and were totally excluded from the rise in prosperity during the Victorian era. Owen's father William Henry fits firmly into this tradition. Having become an estate painter by the time of his marriage he continued in this trade until his retirement, being fortunate enough to work for a wealthy family who provided retirement cottages for superannuated staff.

For at least a century before his birth, and probably for many previous centuries, Owen's paternal ancestors had worked on the land. They generally lacked any formal education and remained illiterate, making their 'mark' on official documents when required to do so. Through his education, achieved only through considerable personal efforts, Owen would succeed in breaking free from this traditional environment, though at the cost of severing the relationship with his father and brothers.

2.01 The Miller's Tale – Marjorie's Maternal Ancestors

Owen offered nothing in the way of family background or ofinancial prospects to recommend him to Harry and Emily Vicker as a desirable suitor for the hand of their only daughter Marjorie Mary, born on 4th

January 1907 in Elmbridge Road, an affluent area of the City of Gloucester. One grandfather, a City Councillor and Alderman, was the proprietor of a popular and prosperous grocery store. Her other grandfather, who had died 15 years earlier, had been a successful miller and farmer, and also a City Councillor. Both were prominent in the local Masonic community.

Marjorie's mother was born Emily Mary Luker on 9th January 1882. We can trace her family back to Emily's great grandfather John Luker (1793-1853), born probably on 3rd November 1793, six weeks after the marriage of his parents Thomas and Martha. Thomas Luker (1765-1834) was baptised in Barnsley, 3 miles outside Cirencester, on 2nd October 1765 and married Martha Howes in the same village on 22nd September 1793. He was buried in the nearby village of Bibury on 27th December 1834, and had probably moved there with his wife and their ten children to work at the Arlington Mill.

Martha Howes (1774-1861) was baptised at Castle Eaton hear Highworth in Wiltshire on 29th May 1774, just over 5 weeks after the marriage of her parents John and Mary Howse (sic). She continued to live in Arlington after the loss of her husband whom she survived by nearly 27 years up to the time of her death from old age on 22nd August 1861. At the time of the 1841 census she was living with her unmarried son George and 10 years later, now recorded as a pauper, her unmarried daughter Ann had also moved into her house, together with 2 grandsons aged 10 and 8.

I have traced no conclusive evidence on Thomas's parents William and Mary Luker. Information from other genealogists suggest that Thomas was born in or near Cirencester on 23 July 1732, married Mary Bartlett on 26th September 1763, and died in Cirencester on 8th May 1793. He may have worked as a miller at the Arlington mill. According to this source his parents were Stephen Luker (1685-1765) and Rebecca Packer (1694-1768), but again I have found no documentary evidence to support this ancestry. A possible father to Stephen Luker is another Stephen, a blacksmith in Crudwell outside Cirencester, who married Hannah Stockwell on 26th November 1684. Hannah was a widow from the neighbouring village of Estcot (Eastcourt). To show his classical learning the priest recorded the marriage in Latin – "Stephanus Looker labor ferrarii duxit uxorem

Hannam Stockwell viduam Est.cot vicesimo sexto die Novembris". Looking further back Marjorie maintained that she had Irish blood and it is possible that the Luker family lived in the south of Ireland before migrating to Gloucestershire.

A personal note by Don Luker dated 15th April 2010 on www.francisfrith.com records that his great-great-great-grandfather John Luker was apprenticed in 1805 to Thomas Poole at the Arlington Mill in Bibury for a period of 9 years and 9 months. Don Luker suggests that this was the start of the long Luker family involvement in the Gloucestershire milling trade. As noted above however it is possible that John's grandfather William had also worked as a miller in Bibury which, if correct, suggests that Thomas Luker (son of William and father of John) also followed this family trade. Arlington Mill itself had a very long history, being mentioned in the Domesday Book; after some changes of use it was rebuilt as a corn mill in the 18th century.

This reconstruction of the Luker family history is necessarily tentative, but I see no reason to doubt that John Luker was born in late 1793 into a family of agricultural labourers living in Bibury and other villages just outside Cirencester. The IGI index records Lukers in Bibury back to the first half of the 17th century. John married Esther (or Ester, or Hester) Clift (1791-1865) in Minchinhampton on 20th March 1814. Esther probably came from a similar background to her husband. She was illiterate, in common with several other members of Marjorie's and Owen's ancestors. Illiteracy may go some way to explain the variations in the spelling of names, as census and other forms would have been written down by others on their behalf, going simply by the sound of what they heard. John and Esther had at least 8 children, the oldest probably being Samuel who was baptised in Rodborough, Stroud on 12th March 1815.

John Luker is a key person in this family history. He started the process which, over three generations, resulted in his grandson becoming a respected merchant and City Councillor in the county town of Gloucester. He was apprenticed to the milling trade as an eleven year old boy. If he served his full time as an apprentice he would have completed his term in late 1814 or in 1815. This would have left him free to take up employment elsewhere and to start a family of his own. His marriage in March 1814 suggests that he may have completed his apprenticeship by that date, and the birth of Samuel in Rodborough is a clear indication that he had by then moved to Wallbridge Mill on the Stroudwater Canal on the outskirts of Stroud. The end of apprenticeship coupled with marriage and the move to a new employer mirror the rites of passage in the old English song *Sally in our Alley*:

But when my seven long years are out,
O then I'll marry Sally,
O then we'll wed and then we'll bed
But not in our Alley.

John Luker settled in Rodborough for many years. The 1841 census finds him working as a miller at the Wallbridge Mill and his son Samuel similarly employed at the nearby Dudbridge Mill. As they were employees, not proprietors, this may not sound too significant. An initial observation however is that they were not agricultural labourers, employed on a casual basis as work was available, but skilled workers with permanent employment and probably better pay and conditions. A visit to the Museum in the Park in Stroud tells us much more. A central exhibit in the Museum is a large, sadly anonymous, painting of the Wallbridge area around 1800. It is a fully industrial landscape typical of the early Industrial Revolution. Wallbridge Mill, somewhat in the background, is one of several substantial factories engaged in manufacturing large lengths of cloth for military uniforms. The red, white and blue lengths of newly made cloth are seen stretched out to dry. This complex of factories was a major supplier to the British Army and Navy, and no doubt provided many of the uniforms worn on the battlefields of the Napoleonic Wars. In Letter IV of his *Tour through the Whole Island of Great Britain* Daniel Defoe records that "the manufacture of white cloth was planted in Stroud Water in Gloucestershire, for the sake of the excellent water there for the dying scarlets, and all colours that are dyed in grain, which are better dyed there, than in any other place of England, some towns near London excepted". The decision by John and Samuel Luker to work there shows that they were committed to excellence in new technology and to a future based on industry rather than on the land.

In the light of this their next move may appear surprising. In 1844 or 1845 they took a tenancy of Grove Mill, otherwise known as Marlings Mill after its owner. The mill lay just outside Painswick, on the Painswick Stream. This was a much smaller water-powered corn mill with a supplementary steam engine. It must however have required a fair amount of work. The 1851 census shows 4 millers at work, John and his fourth son William (aged 23), and Samuel and his son John (aged 13). What is probably as significant is that they have become self-employed by setting up a family business. Milling, with the inevitable risk of lung disease, may not however have benefited the health of the Luker family. In the three preceding generations Stephen had reached the age of 90, his son William 60 or 61, and his grandson Thomas (John's father) 70. John Luker died on 17th March 1853 at the age of 59. His widow Esther went to live with her daughter, also Esther, now married to John Land, a grocer in Huntley. She died in October 1865, aged about 75.

Samuel (1815-1867), the eldest son of John and Esther, married Elizabeth Sparrow (1817-1865) in Minchinhampton on 20th August 1836. They had at least 9 children, 5 sons and 4 daughters. After his father's death Samuel and Elizabeth stayed on at Grove Mill until Christmas 1858 when the lease expired. No doubt Samuel could have renewed the lease, but he chose instead to become a tenant of the much larger and more modern Quay Street Mills in Gloucester Docks. This marked a return to industrial scale milling, the mill itself now being entirely steam-powered rather than water-driven. The repeal of the Corn Laws had opened the way to an important import trade in corn, and the opening of the Gloucester and Sharpness Canal had for the first time allowed large ships to sail right up to Gloucester, rather than having to unload their cargoes into smaller boats lower down the river. Gloucester had become a major hub for the import of corn destined for the Midlands, with corn coming into the port from the Continent and from Ireland. Samuel Luker also appears to have taken the lease of the Island Street Mills and possibly of the Victoria Street Mills. The opening of the domestic market to imported corn provided Samuel Luker with an important commercial opening of which he took full advantage. It also contributed to an agricultural depression in England and to downward pressure on agricultural wages. So that what benefited the Luker family would have had a negative impact on Owen's ancestors.

By 1861 Samuel and Elizabeth were living at Quay Street with several children, including one married son with his wife and child. Elizabeth however died on 23rd November 1865 and less than five months later on 4th April 1866 Samuel celebrated his second marriage with Mary Ann Hawkins of Longhope, the widowed daughter of Stephen Hayward, a veterinary surgeon. He was not however able to enjoy this new-found domestic happiness for very long since he died in Barnwood on 11th December 1867. The causes of death were given as the softening of the base of the brain, and an abdominal abscess. Aged 52, he died even younger than his father had done. The Probate record states:

> *The Testator Samuel Luker was formerly of Quay Street in the Parish of Saint Nicholas in the City of Gloucester, Miller and Publican, but late of the Parish of Barnwood in the City of Gloucester, Miller and Corn Dealer, and died on the 11th day of December 1867 at the Parish of Barnwood aforesaid.*

In his will, made on 26th September 1866, he had appointed his new wife Mary Ann as his executrix and bequeathed to her the benefit of a life assurance policy in the sum of five hundred pounds. That he did not specify any property in his will strongly suggests that he was still a lessee rather than a mill owner.

How Samuel's milling interests were split on his death is not entirely clear. One son, James, was granted a 14 year lease of mills in Quay Street at a rent of £35 per annum. The previous occupant was John Gregory. It is noted that James Luker was already in occupation, and had installed a steam boiler and other milling equipment. James died on 14th April 1882 but, according to an affidavit made by his eldest child Florence Austin, the property was still held by his widow Eleanor as late as 1908. Another son, John (1838-1902), took over the property known as the Quay Street Mills, subsequently being declared bankrupt in *The London Gazette* of 14th September 1875. The official notice describes him as follows:

> *In the Matter of a Special Resolution for Liquidation by Arrangement of the affairs of John Luker, of the Quay Steam*

Mills, and the Duke Inn, Quay-street, in the city of Gloucester, Miller, Corn Merchant, and Innkeeper.[3]

Both Samuel Luker and his son John had diversified their businesses to expand into trading as corn merchants and innkeepers. Given the scale of the corn trade through Gloucester the move into the business of corn merchants, perhaps initially on a small scale, was a natural development. And there were several pubs in the dockland area, catering both for local workers and for the crews of ships berthed in the port. It was inevitably a pretty rough part of town. Marjorie recalled her father saying that policemen always went there in pairs, and that wealthy men kept their mistresses down there – no doubt a euphemism for the prostitution often associated with such areas. Clearly however drink and sex sold well and the Luker family were well placed to capitalise on the drinking and to turn a blind eye to what went on in the rooms upstairs. We should remember that, for all its official prudery, the late Victorian age was notorious for the level of prostitution, with thousands of women plying their trade on the streets of London alone.

It was Samuel Luker's fourth son, Henry Charles (1844-1892), who took over the Island Street Mills. Born on 16th October 1844 he married Sarah Louisa Farley (1841-1931) on 4th June 1868. Sarah, born on 9th March 1841, was the daughter of Job Farley, a hosier in Camden Town, and his wife Harriet. Job Farley (c.1812-c.1855) was born around 1812, probably in Worcester, and moved to work as a hosier in London where he married Harriet Costins (1816-1849) on 4th September 1831 in St Pancras Church. Harriet had been born in 1816 so was only 15 years old at the time of the marriage. In 1841 they were living in Archer Street, St Pancras with their 2 daughters, Emma (born 1835) and Sarah Louisa (born 1841). Harriet died in 1849 so by 1851 Job Farley was a widower and living at the Model Lodging House, King Street, St Giles in the Fields. It is likely that he died in the following decade. I have not traced Emma in the records beyond 1841 but in 1851 and 1861 Sarah Louisa was living in Upton on Severn with Elijah and Mary Farmer, being shown first as a visitor and

---

3 I am assuming that this John Luker is Samuel's son, born in 1838. He might however be Samuel's brother, born in 1834 and the youngest child of John and Esther Luker.

later as a niece. At the time of her marriage to Henry Luker she is shown as resident in Eldwrsfield.

Henry Charles, like his father Samuel, diversified his business interests, moving to Parlours Farm in Minsterworth while continuing his trade as a master miller. Henry and Sarah had at least 11 children, as follows:

Ellen Elizabeth	1869	Henry	1879
Louisa Alice	1870	Stroud Lucy	1880
Henry Albert	1873	Emily Mary	1882
Esther Annie	1874	Tom	1884
Lewis George	1875	May	1886
Frank	1878		

Tragedy however struck the family in 1876 when 3 children, Louisa, Henry and Lewis died in the space of a few weeks. On 3rd May Henry Albert succumbed to malignant scarlet fever. Then on 23rd August Lewis George died of infantile cholera, and on the same day Louisa Alice succumbed to brain disease, described as arachnitis combined with a stroke and an effusion into the ventricle of the brain. And on 5th February 1892 Ellen Elizabeth, the beloved eldest sister and mainstay of the family, died at the early age of 23 from heart disease and serous effusions in brain. With both Samuel Luker and 2 of his grandchildren succumbing to brain disease there may have been some hereditary medical condition affecting the family. Also in 1892 Henry Luker died on 25th May at the young age of 47, having suffered coronary thrombosis caused by a fatty heart. The Gloucester Journal for 28th May gave a report of his death:

> *Mr Luker, who was an ardent Liberal, for many years sat in the Gloucester Chamber as one of the representatives of the West Ward. He was elected in 1881, 1884 and 1887 and did not stand in the 1890 election. He was Guardian of the Gloucester Union and a Freemason, being Past Senior Warden of the Zetland Lodge (No 1,000) and a Past Provost, also Grand Steward of Gloucestershire.*

His widow, Sarah Louisa, was to live on in the Gloucester area for nearly 40 years more, dying on 17th November 1931 at the age of 90.

Unlike her husband she was therefore able to celebrate the marriages of their children. One marriage she may not have welcomed however was that of their fourth child Esther Annie, about whom there is some mystery.

Esther Annie was born on 18th July 1874. She was therefore around 2 years old when her 3 siblings died in the annus horriblis of 1876. It would not be surprising if that experience scarred her for life. At the age of 6 or 7, when the 1881 census was taken, she was living with her younger brother Frank at the house of the farm bailiff. There is nothing surprising in this. Their mother Sarah had recently given birth to her seventh child Stroud Lucy and was also looking after Henry, who would have been under two years old. However the 1891 census records Annie living as a boarder at Holywell College in Weston-super-Mare. There was no tradition in the Luker family of private education or of boarding schools, and the only reasonable inference is that Annie, by now 16 years old, was proving to be a very troublesome teenager. We pick up her story on 14th April 1898 when she married Benjamin Joseph Surman, the son of a farmer called William Surman. Ben Surman, two years older than Annie, was working as a miller's clerk, presumably at one of the mills leased by the Luker family. It is possible that the marriage met with parental disapproval from both families, as no family members acted as witnesses at the ceremony in the Gloucester Register Office. Ben and Annie were to have two daughters, Nancy and Nellie, born in Gloucester in 1900 and 1901 respectively[4]. According to the 1911 census Nancy and Nellie were the only 2 children of Ben and Annie's marriage. Annie was then living with the children on a farm owned by her brother Frank and his wife Eliza near Newport in South Wales.
On 8th August of the same year Annie drowned in the River Severn at Tewkesbury, the coroner's inquest on the following

[4] Brian and Garry Wood note the birth on 3rd June 1898 of a girl, Bessie Cecilia Surman. Without sight of the birth certificate they assume Bessie to have been Esther's daughter, conceived some months before marriage and (in their view) to a different father. There is nothing in this. Both the birth and death certificates for Bessie Cecilia (she died in March 1899 at the age of 9 months) show her as the daughter of Henry Charles Surman, an innkeeper from Cheltenham, and his wife Elizabeth. There may have been a family relationship, but Bessie Cecilia was not Annie's daughter.

day finding that she had committed suicide while in an unsound state of mind. She is described as a 'probationer, housewife of Ben Surman, a miller'. The description 'probationer' suggests that she had got into trouble with the law, and it is possible that this was the immediate cause of her suicide. There is no mention of Ben Surman in the 1911 UK census. On 5th January of that year he had sailed from London to Wellington, New Zealand on the RMSS Corinthic of the Shaw Savill line. He was travelling by himself as an unaccompanied male. The identification is confirmed by his description as a 'miller'. The other passengers were also workers emigrating in search of a new life overseas. It is likely that he was emigrating with assistance provided by the New Zealand government. We do not know whether Benjamin emigrated because his marriage had irretrievably broken down, or whether he hoped to ask his wife and children to follow him once he had secured employment in New Zealand. Annie's suicide later in the same year suggests that she was convinced that the separation was permanent.

The National Probate Calendar for 1932 shows limited administration of Annie's estate granted to Frank Luker, who is also described as attorney of Benjamin Joseph Surman. Why it should have taken 21 years to reach this stage, with an estate worth only £453 15s 2d is unclear. Ben Surman was probably still alive, and may be the Benjamin Surman who, according to Australian death records, died in Perth in 1964 at the age of 87.

I have suggested that Ben and Annie's marriage may have incurred parental disapproval. However it is interesting to note that in a 1919 trade directory the firm of Luker & Surman Ltd is advertised as the proprietors of the Island Steam Mills in Lower Westgate Street. There cannot therefore have been a total breach between the Luker and Surman families. The commitment to new technology remains in evidence; out of over 70 mills listed for Gloucestershire Luker & Surman Ltd is one of only 2 businesses to give a telephone number (Gloucester 212). This was however almost the end of the Luker family's interest in milling, as the business was sold in the following year to the West Midlands Agricultural Co-operative Society.

Emily Mary Luker ((1882-1976), the ninth child of this rather troubled family, would marry Harry James Vicker on 2nd January 1906 and they would become Marjorie's parents. Another of Emily's sisters, Stroud Lucy (always known as Lucy), emigrated to Argentina in May 1909 to work as a teacher. She stayed there until at least December 1935, returning to England for 10 weeks in 1921 and for a mere 12 days in 1930. Having lost 4 older siblings through death, one through suicide, and another through emigration, Emily Mary Luker no doubt found it especially hard to accept her Marjorie's decision to emigrate to China in 1934.

2.02 The Vicker Family – Marjorie's Paternal Ancestors

Marjorie was born on 4th January 1907 in Elmbridge Road, an affluent area of the City of Gloucester. Her immediate background could hardly have been more different than that of Owen. Her father Harry James Vicker worked as manager in the family firm of J G Vicker & Co, long established grocers, provision merchants and wine merchants trading from substantial premises in Westgate Street, the prime shopping area of the city. The history of this firm was researched in 1953 by a Mr Brian Smith of Weston Road, Gloucester on behalf of Marjorie's brother Arthur Vicker:

THE HISTORY OF J G VICKER & CO LTD
At the sign of the Golden Grasshopper

> There is an old story, long disproved, that the origin of the sign of the Grasshopper lay in the incident where some merchant seamen, laden with tea from India, had their lives saved when, lost in a thick fog, they knew they were near land when they heard the loud chirping of grasshoppers. This story was connected with the romantic story of the life of the great sixteenth century merchant grocer, Sir Thomas Gresham, who founded the Royal Exchange. It has been shown, however, that the grasshopper was a crest in use in his family as far back as the fifteenth century. In spite of this, the crest has always been used as a sign of a good grocery business, and this has certainly proved to be the case with the present firm.
>
> Many Gloucester establishments had their signs in the streets here in the eighteenth century, but most of them have disappeared. Not so the Grasshopper. We know that it appeared first in connection with the present business as early as October

1791, when the premises were in Northgate Street, opened by one William Holt. There is little doubt but that it is the same golden grasshopper that can be seen today. Mr Holt specialised in tea, and set a high standard of business, "equal in goodness to the first retail shops in London; having had an opportunity of selecting such Teas as cannot fail giving general satisfaction". At this period the only other commodities he chose to advertise were "Sugars, Spices, Starch, Blue, &c., &c."[5]

Six years after the business was set up in Northgate Street, the sign of the Grasshopper was moved to the site it occupied for over 150 years, namely at what was No.4 Westgate Street (later re-numbered as 7). Tea was still his speciality, together with coffee, chocolate and patent cocoa, whilst other goods he advertised consisted of sugars, rice, spices, starch, blue and mustard. Mr Holt continued in business for a good number of years, dying about 1822, after a few years in retirement.

The high standard he had set has continued through its various proprietors, and this is evident in the next to take over the business, a local man who came from an old Hartpury family, Mr Joseph Hooper. He retained both the sign and the quality of the concern. Continuing alone for some years he took another local man as a partner, namely Mr John Bellamy. The resulting firm of Hooper and Bellamy continued as grocers and tea-dealers for many years at No.4 Westgate Street. Mr Hooper acquired a reputation for his 'steady perseverance in upright, honest business habits" so that he was able to retire from the firm to his house, Somerset Cottage, The Spa, where he died the 13th February 1862, aged 72. Mr John Bellamy was the sole

---

[5] Brian Smith enclosed a handwritten transcript of the original advertisement in the Journal of Monday 10th October 1791:

GLOCESTER. TEA WAREHOUSE, At the GRASSHOPPER, NORTHGATE STREET. W Holt most respectfully informs his Friends and the Public, that having laid in a choice stock of TEAS of the first quality, highest flavour, and latest importation, he has opened the above SHOP for the sale of every article in the TEA TRADE, equal in goodness to the first retail shops in London; having had an opportunity of selecting such Teas as cannot fail giving general satisfaction, and determined to pay every attention to the quality of his Teas, he humbly intreats the support of his friends and the public, whose favours he will studiously endeavour to merit.

N.B. Sugars, Spices, Starch, Blue &c &c.

[Author's note: *blue* is an old name for washing powder or liquid]

proprietor for some years, as a "Family Tea Dealer and Grocer", specialising in British wines, pickles, foreign fruits, spices, fish-sauces, hams, tongues, etc". He also opened some new premises in Northgate Street, and eventually took into partnership, in about the year 1870, Mr James Godwin Vicker, and the name of the firm then became "Bellamy & Vicker" with its branch establishment at No.67 Northgate Street. For some forty years Mr Bellamy had retained the firm's high reputation, and he was able to retire from the business in 1879, four years before his death in January 1883.

The firm of "J G Vicker & Co, The Original City and County Supply Stores" went from strength to strength with the passing years, and by 1895 the premises occupied Nos 4 and 5 Westgate Street, as well as their Northgate Street branch. They had taken on a wider range of goods, and these now included such a variety as "Teas, Coffees, General Groceries, Provisions, Wines, Spirits, Ales, Stouts, Patent Medicines, Druggists' Sundries, Stationery, Brushes, Mats, Sponges, and Toilet Requisites".

Today the business is carried on by members of the third generation of the Vicker family, and a private company was formed in 1938 known as J G Vicker & Co Ltd. It has always been their aim to maintain the firm's great reputation, and in this respect they feel that they have even surpassed it. Thus, for well over 160 years that familiar sight to all Gloucestrians, the golden Grasshopper, is now over the doorway of No.9 Westgate Street. It it is still there to see that patrons still get every attention to their wants.

The golden Grasshopper, which can now be seen in the Gloucester Folk Museum, is almost certainly not the original 1791 sign but a later replacement. And, despite Mr Brian Smith's tactful demythologising of the grasshopper story, Marjorie adhered to the family tradition that the sign originated from the discovery of a live grasshopper in a crate of tea shipped from India.

In Kelly's Directory of Gloucestershire for 1902 the firm is listed as follows:

Vicker J G & Co, grocers and provision merchants, & agents for W & A Gilbey Limited, wine & spirit merchants. The Original

City & County Grocery & Provision Supply Stores, 5 Westgate street.

James Godwin's eldest son Ernest Godwin and his third son Harry James had become the joint proprietors of the firm in 1919 following the death of their father. It is unclear why George Sidney, the second son, did not become a member of the partnership; he was involved in the business at the time of the 1911 census and lived in Gloucester until his death in 1950. But the will of Ernest Godwin, who died in 1931, refers simply to his partnership agreement with Harry James. Ernest Godwin's sons did not become partners, and I assume that Harry James agreed with the executors to buy out all other family interests in the firm. When Harry James Vicker died in July 1944 he was therefore able to transfer the entire business to his sons Arthur and John.

As Brian Smith's history makes clear the involvement of the Vicker family in the business had started with Harry's father, James Godwin Vicker (1841-1918), born in Bruton, a village in Somerset on 11th September 1841. James Godwin was the last son of William Vicker (1813-1843), a glazier or plumber, and Mary Eliza Hann (c.1817-1891).

William Vicker was born in Somerset in the parish of Cameley and Temple Cloud where he was baptised on 6th October 1813. His parents were William Vicker (1776-1851) and Priscilla Bamfield (1774-1869), both of whom were born in that parish and who were married there on 6th February 1809. They subsequently moved a few miles away to Bruton where they had at least five further children: George, Charles, Sarah, Eliza, and Priscilla). William Vicker senior is variously described as a carrier, as a farmer, and as a fellmonger who would have prepared animal skins for a tanner. He died in Bruton on 21st February 1851. His wife Priscilla, daughter of Samuel and Rebecca Bamfield, was born in Cameley in 1785 where she was baptised on 9th October. She did not remarry after William's death and spent her final years in the Bruton Almshouses.

William Vicker junior and his wife Mary Eliza married on 9th November 1835 in Gillingham in Dorset. In their short time together as a married couple they had three children, all sons. The eldest, Frank

James, was born in 1836 but died in infancy and is not shown in the 1841 census record The second son Edwin was born in 1839 and James Godwin, Marjorie's grandfather, was born on 11th September 1841. However William Vicker suffered from consumption or tubercolosis and died in Bruton on 23rd December 1843 when he was only 30 years old.

As Marjorie's grandmother Mary Eliza Vicker is important to the family history. Her own life was scarred by tragedy and is of some interest in itself. The consistent evidence of the census records is that she was born in Gosport around 1816 and it is very probable that she was the daughter of James Hann and Martha Godwin who were married in Portsea in 1814. It is perhaps significant that she named her third son James Godwin Vicker and also that later census records show Martha Hann living back with her family in Gillingham in Dorset after losing her husband. Most records relating to the Hann family come from Gillingham, but the presence of James Hann in Portsea in 1814 may arise from his involvement in the Napoleonic wars. Was he volunteered or press-ganged for naval service and if so was he the James Hann shown in British military records as a private on HMS Excellent, a 74 gun third rate man of war that took part in the battle of Cape St Vincent in 1797 and in the suppression of a revolt by the 8th West India Regiment in Dominica in 1802? The West India Regiments were recruited mainly from black Caribbean slaves purchased from the plantations and the spark for the short-lived revolt of the 8th Regiment was the fear that they would be used effectively as slave labour in the sugar cane fields. The military records show that James Hann received his discharge from naval service in 1810. If he was indeed Marjorie's great grandfather then he would be the only known ancestor in any branch of our family to have seen active military service or to have actively participated in the maintenance of the slave economy of the British empire. There may of course be others who benefited many different ways from the existence of the empire.

I have mentioned above that Mary Eliza lost her eldest child in infancy and that her husband William Vicker then died at age of 30 after only eight years of marriage. Mary Eliza remained single for some years but on 21st July 1851 she married Alfred Ferrett, her first husband's apprentice who had probably kept the business going after William's death. Alfred was only 25 at the time of the wedding, a full ten years younger than his new wife, but this marriage was to last less than twelve weeks since Alfred died in October of the same year from inflammation of the brain, leaving Mary Eliza pregnant with her fourth and last child. This daughter Fanny Blanch was born on 3rd December and must therefore have been conceived several months before her marriage to Alfred.

After the death of her second husband Mary Ferrett lived as a widow at Coombe Street in Bruton where she worked as a dressmaker and subsequently ran the village grocery shop. In 1871, now 55 years old, she was living with her elder son Edwin at the Stapleton Arms pub in Buckhorn Weston near Wincanton in Dorset. Subsequently she moved to Station Road in Gillingham and is recorded as living on interest. Her daughter Fanny, still unmarried, was living at the same address in 1881. Mary Eliza remained living in Station Road until her death in 1891.

The 1861 census shows Edwin Vicker, then aged 22, living in Newbury near Shaftesbury in Dorset with his uncle and aunt William and Caroline Hann, their six children, and his widowed grandmother Martha Hann. William Hann worked as a butcher and Edwin was working in his business. At some time in the following decade he moved to the Stapleton Arms in Buckhorn Weston where he carried on trade as a butcher and innkeeper. An article in the Western Gazette and Flying Post for Friday 24th May 1872 suggests that he and his mother Mary Eliza were popular residents taking a full part in village life:

> Young Men's Friendly Society – The anniversary of this excellent Society was held on Monday last. The inhabitants of the village seemed determined to enjoy themselves, although the weather was very unfavourable. The bells rang merry peals during the day. The members assembled at 11 o'clock, and marched to church, where an address was delivered by the Rector, the Rev H Stapleton. Afterwards, they adjourned to the Stapleton Arms Inn, where an excellent repast awaited them, provided by the worthy host and hostess, Mr Edwin Vicker and his mother, in their usual good style. After the removal of the cloth, the usual loyal toasts were drunk, and six fresh members were added to the list.

This picture of a popular and successful local trader is however misleading. In his bankruptcy hearing in January 1895 Edwin admitted that he had been trading since 1873 while knowingly insolvent. By submitting his bankruptcy petition and admitting his previous insolvency he had unwittingly exposed himself to prosecution for fraud and the Shepton Mallet Journal for Friday 14th June 1895 gives a full account of the resulting trial;

> Edwin Vicker, 56, butcher, on bail, was indicted for unlawfully obtaining, four months before his bankruptcy, by means of a worthless cheque, from Christopher Mullins Moody, two bullocks on credit, at Evercreech, on October 3rd, 1894. Mr Garland, who was briefed for the prosecution, called Mr C M Moody, auctioneer, carrying on business at Evercreech. He stated that on October 4th, he conducted a sale at that town, which defendant attended and bought two bullocks, for which he tendered a cheque for £33 10s. The cheque was dishonoured, and witness had never received payment for the animals. Mr Frederick E T Fowler, manager of Stuckey's bank at Wincanton, deposed that on the 1st October, prisoner's account was over-drawn to the extent of £29 8s, and he told him he must not draw any more on the bank. On the 6th October the cheque in question was presented, and he declined to cash it. Further evidence as to the prisoner's bankruptcy having been given, prisoner addressed the court and said that he had no intention of defrauding Mr Moody, as he anticipated that sufficient money would be paid into the bank to meet the cheque. He had had an account at Stuckey's Wincanton Bank for 14 years, and they had allowed him to overdraw. He had during that time paid them £745 for interest on overdrafts. The jury found the prisoner guilty, and the judge, in sentencing him, said that he did not regard his offence as a very bad one, though of course it was very hard upon the owner of the fat beasts to lose his money for those beasts; but on the other hand he did not think prisoner did it in order to put it into his own pocket. (Prisoner: "I did not"). He (the learned judge) dared say prisoner was in hopes that, as his bankers had the guarantee, they would prove softer hearted than they did. No doubt, if he had known that by being made a bankrupt he was turning what he had done into a criminal offence, he would not have presented his petition. He did not regard it as a very bad case, because it was not like that of a debtor who, just before his bankruptcy went and put

goods on credit to put them away for better times, and therefore he (the learned judge) was going to deal leniently with him. He held in his hands a medical certificate, certifying that he was incapable of any physical strain. During the time he was in prison proper care would be taken of him, and he would not be asked to undergo and labour or deprivation of food likely to affect his health. This would not be so, even if he did not give special instructions to that effect; but he did so now. He sentenced prisoner to one month's imprisonment without hard labour.

The crucial step in the life of James Godwin Vicker (1841-1919) was his move to Gloucester, and the start of his employment in John Bellamy's shop. There is no definite information about when or why he left home or how he came to settle in Gloucester where there were no obvious family connections. By the time of the 1861 census, when he was 19 years old, he was working at the shop in Gloucester. He married Kate Smith, the attractive daughter of a farmer in Taynton, on 3rd August 1869 and became a partner in the business in the following year. In 1879, on Bellamy's retirement, he took over the entire business. He remained the sole proprietor of the firm for 40 years.

Kate Smith (1847-1918) was the fourth daughter of Thomas Smith and his wife Anne Pope Ford who were married in Taynton on 5th March 1835. Anne Pope Ford (1813-1786) was the eldest daughter of a farming family since her father Daniel Ford (1788-1862) had farmed in Upleadon with his wife Ann Ford (1791-1877). It was not unusual for young farmers to marry the daughters of neighbouring farmers since girls brought up on the farm well knew the routines and challenges of farming life. By marrying James Godwin Vicker Anne's daughter Kate Smith would leave the farming community to join the commercial élite in the city of Gloucester. Anne Pope's husband Thomas Smith farmed 170 acres at Haynes Farm in Taynton and employed four men and one boy as well no doubt as receiving regular help from family members. He died, probably in 1860,but his widow Anne Pope continued to run the farm for 12 or more years although with a reduction in size to 100 acres and a consequent reduction to two employees. By 1881 she had retired to Church Street in Newent where she died in early 1886.

There were 9 children from the marriage of James Godwin Vicker and Kate Smith:

Ernest	1871	Lilian	1880
George Sidney	1873	Hugh Cecil	1882
Florence K	1875	Hilda Muriel	1884
Harry James	1876	Edith May	1893
Gertrude	1879		

With the exception of the youngest child Edith May, who died in the year of her birth, all their children survived into adulthood and were still alive at the date of the 1911 census. This is in stark contrast with the tragic record of the Luker family.

On 1st May 1918 he lost his wife Kate, by then living at Kingsdown House in Box in Wiltshire. Kingsdown House had been a well known madhouse, but by the early 20th century had become a respectable private sanatorium charging quite high fees. Kate suffered from chronic bronchitis and either this physical condition, or a possible onset of dementia, would have prompted her move to Kingsdown House. James Godwin survived his wife for just over 15 months, dying suddenly in August 1919. Although he had been ill he had appeared to make a satisfactory recovery and was still at work. He attended to the business all day on Wednesday 13th August and then on the morning of Thursday 14th August, returning home as usual for dinner. In the afternoon however he felt unwell, lay down to rest and died at 6.15pm. He had become a pillar of the local establishment, a long time Councillor and Alderman of the City, a Justice of the Peace and Past President of the Gloucester Chamber of Trade. He was also President of the Gloucester Grocers' Association and an enthusiastic supporter of the Gloucester Root, Fruit and Grain Society. His death was announced in the Gloucester Journal of 16th August 1919. In the same issue the Journal reported the death of Mr Andrew Carnegie, "Steel-master, Multi-millionaire, and Philanthropist", and advertised a new show at the Palace Theatre, Gloucester – "A Chinese Honeymoon" with music by Howard Talbot and words by George Dance, as played for 1200 performances at the Strand Theatre, 'the Funniest Musical Comedy ever Written'". For James Godwin Vicker, and for the rest of his family (not least Marjorie herself) it would have seemed incredible that his granddaughter would be enjoying her honeymoon in China a mere 15 years later.

Marjorie and her two brothers were born into very comfortable circumstances. Her parents would undoubtedly have taken pride in the success of the family, very probably with some element of Victorian self-righteousness in the thought that the failure of others to achieve similar success was a consequence of their own failings or lack of moral fibre. It is however worth emphasising how recently they had acquired financial security and respectability. On the Luker side this derived from the decision of Samuel Luker to move from Painswick to Gloucester in 1859. The Luker family, who had suffered family tragedies and the bankruptcy of family members, would have been particularly aware of the narrow dividing line between success and failure. On the Vicker side Marjorie's grandfather James Godwin had managed in his own lifetime to progress from humble beginnings in Bruton to commercial and political success in the City of Gloucester. No doubt all members of the family were aware that what had been so recently gained could quite easily be lost again, and that all members of the family had the duty to do their utmost to maintain and consolidate the position that they had acquired. Marjorie had a very strong sense of family duty, but at the end of the day chose to marry a man whom her father could not accept as a proper husband for her. In so doing she went against the family expectation that she would marry into the commercial and civic elite of the city and thus do her bit to strengthen the position of the family.

2.03 Marjorie's Parents – Harry James Vicker & Emily Mary Luker

On 2nd January 1906 Harry James Vicker and Emily Mary Luker were married in the Parish Church of St Mary de Lode in the City of Gloucester. The witnesses to the marriage were Harry's father James Godwin, Emily's mother Sarah Louisa and Emily's brother Frank. The newly married couple took up residence in a property known as Kennerleigh in Elmbridge Road, a highly respectable area about a mile from the city centre. It was there that Marjorie, their eldest child, was born on 4th January 1907, and she was subsequently baptised at St Mary de Lode in the church which had seen the wedding of her parents. Her 2 brothers, Arthur and John, were born in 1909 and 1915. Marjorie would, unlike Owen, have known and been close to 3 of her 4 grandparents. The family was also sufficiently wealthy to employ one or more servants, a 17 year girl called Nora Vaile being resident in Elmbridge Road in 1911.

At some stage the family moved to 31 Heathville Road, and then at the end of 1937 to the property known as Rose Mede or 43 Heathville Road (the property at 31 Heathville Road being transferred to their younger son John). Rose Mede remained the beloved family home for many years and, after Harry James's death in 1944, Emily Mary continued to reside there until January 1952 when she moved to a smaller property at 66 Estcourt Road. She still employed a servant to help with housework and cooking. By 1967 or 1968 she was no longer able to live by herself and moved in with Owen and Marjorie at the Rectory in Moreton-in-the-Marsh where she lived until Owen's retirement in the auturmn of 1970. It did not make life easier that, after a lifetime of living with servants, she expected Marjorie to be at her beck and call. She also retained highly traditional views, expressing concern about the US space programme on the grounds that man was trespassing on God's territory. When Owen retired in 1970 she moved to a nursing home in Gloucester and, physically frail but mentally fully alert, lived there until her death in 1976 at the age of 94.

CHAPTER 3

THE ROAD TO CHINA

Childhood and Youth

Being born in comfortable circumstances provides no guarantee against misfortune, and at the age of four Marjorie was struck down with polio. She was left with a permanently withered and partially paralysed right arm, being able to use her right hand only by first lifting the weak arm with her good left hand. Her education however proceeded smoothly. She attended the Denmark Road High School for Girls and became Head Girl in her final year. In 1924 she passed her School Certificate in 7 subjects: Religious Knowledge, English (with distinction), English History, Geography, Latin, French & Spoken French, and Drawing. Two years later, in 1926, she obtained her Higher School Certificate in French and History, with Latin and Shakespeare as subsidiary subjects. The headmistress at the time was E Penson, who provided Marjorie with a job reference on 31st January 1930 in support of her application to work at the PNEU head office in Ambleside:

> Miss Marjorie Vicker was a pupil at this School for a number of years. She was a girl of good ability and great diligence. She obtained her School Certificate and then did two years' advanced work leading up to a second examination. After which she went on to the University and took an honours degree in History.
> Miss Vicker's greatest asset is her reliability. She is methodical and businesslike, and also possesses that far-reaching power of seeing what needs to be done and doing it without commotion. I have had experience of this, myself, when she held office here as Head Girl. She has a quick mind, but will not be ashamed to learn her new work, and when she has learnt it, she will not be afraid to take up her responsibilities.
> I am sure that Miss Vicker would make a very efficient secretary and I know that she would be a most trustworthy one. She is pleasant in manner and appearance.

On finishing school Marjorie went to Bristol University to study history. A well educated and very attractive girl she was clearly cut out as a highly eligible match for any young bachelor in the commercial elite of the city of Gloucester. Going to university was not part of the family tradition, and it was still unusual for girls to study for a degree. Probably this was her personal decision, with the support of her parents who were well able to support her financially through her years at college.

By contrast Owen grew up in The Old House in Queenhill where he had been born in 1901. The property still stands on the corner of two lanes in this quiet hamlet; the hamlet itself and the roads leading to it have changed little in the last century. The Old House is now in single occupation but, as noted in the previous chapter, the present owner states that it was originally divided into three units. Owen began his education at the local Dame School, no doubt in what is now the Old School House immediately across the lane from his home, and attended the village school in Bushley, 3 miles down the road past the Dowdeswell seat at Pull Court. He must have done well there since he won a scholarship to Tewkesbury Grammar School, there being only 4 such scholarships on offer to boys living outside the town. This school, with a history dating back to Elizabethan days, had in 1906 moved into new purpose-built premises opposite the Abbey, where it stayed until 1952. The school records held in the Gloucestershire Archives show that he was admitted to the school in September 1914. Queenhill is only a few miles from Tewkesbury and within easy cycling distance for a fit young man with an interest in sports, and there is little doubt that Owen commuted daily to and from the school. Throughout his youth Owen also manifested a keen desire for academic achievement, and it is likely that he did well at Tewkesbury Grammar. However the son of a village labourer could not reasonably expect to prolong his education or aspire to university entrance, and in February 1917 he left school in order to take up wartime employment in the BSA (British Small Arms) munitions factory in Birmingham. The fact that he left half way through the school term perhaps indicates that a family disagreement had come to a head, with Owen feeling that it was better for him to leave home and make his own way in life.

The school syllabus comprised English, History, Mathematics, Chemistry, Physics, Botany, Nature Study, Latin and French. Both botany and nature study involved outdoor work and the observations of plants in the country. *The Lay of the Last Minstrel* by Walter Scott formed the introduction to English Literature, with later reading being determined by the texts set for study by the Cambridge Local Examination Board. It may well have been in those English lessons that Owen acquired his love of literature, and the school no doubt left its mark on him in other ways.

Owen's employment at BSA Munitions was essential war work and no doubt Owen took this job pending his anticipated call up for military service. While in Birmingham he lodged with the YMCA (Young Men's Christian Association), and it was probably there that he first sensed his vocation for the priesthood. Almost certainly he started on the night classes that led to the Higher School Certificate, a necessary qualification for further study. His second son Anthony recalled him acknowledging the support and encouragement that he received from his Scoutmaster to continue his academic studies and to qualify himself for professional employment.

When the war ended Owen continued to work in Birmingham as an employee of Thacker & Co, a stationery firm based in Cornwall Street. According to the 1921 census he was living as a lodger at 90 May Lane, King's Heath, the home of George and Sarah Thistlewood. However an attack of measles with severe complications led his doctor to recommend that he took outdoor employment. Quite probably unhealthy conditions of work in the munitions factory had damaged his lungs as a result of prolonged exposure to dangerous chemicals. He therefore returned to the family home at Queenhill and took up work as a labourer in the market gardens of Pull Court, thus joining his father and eldest brother Victor in the employment of the Dowdeswell family. This apparent setback laid the foundation for his lifelong love of gardening, particularly the useful cultivation of vegetables and fruit rather than the decorative tending of flowers. This was a solid apprenticeship for a man who from 1945 to 1970 was to live in vicarages and rectories with extensive grounds requiring continual maintenance. Working on a big estate would also have brought home to him the economic and social gap between the wealthy owners and the labourers in the grounds. Throughout his life he was never wholly comfortable in the company of those higher up the social scale. In this he experienced the common penalty of upward social mobility, being comfortable neither in the class into which he was born nor in that to which he had progressed. He was always most at ease in the work environment with other parsons and on the sports field. Marjorie's background was of course among the social elite of Gloucester and if, as is quite possible, she did visit the Dowdeswell family in the company of her father or grandfather then she would have been in the drawing-room looking out over the gardens and the anonymous gardeners.

Life at home cannot have been entirely easy. The family was poor. Owen recalled trapping rabbits to supplement the basic diet. Queenhill was also somewhat remote from the outside world, and one of his earliest memories, no doubt from his pre-war childhood, was that of seeing his first aeroplane and chasing it across the field in the belief that it was a strange bird. In other ways too there were obvious tensions. While Owen remained close to his mother throughout her life relations with his father were always more difficult. The immediate cause was his father's drinking. How serious this was cannot now be known. There is no evidence that it interfered with his father's performance of his duties as an estate painter, since a man found to be drunk in charge of a paintbrush might expect short shrift from his employer. There is no evidence either that it affected his overall health, since he lived to the age of 74, dying in 1941 of a stroke. More probably William Henry drank heavily at the weekend and arrived home drunk and possibly violent. Owen, not always tactful in his interventions, made his views known and simply widened the rift between them. He was himself to live as a teetotaller for some years, although he came to enjoy a modest social drink and, in later life, a fairly regular nightcap.

Another cause of the rift with his father was Owen's obvious desire to make a better life for himself, perhaps already manifested in his leaving home to work in Birmingham. While working on the estate gardens he continued his studies for the school certificate examinations and in 1924 gained admission to St Boniface Missionary College in Warminster. His decision to follow his vocation as a clergyman appears to have been the final break with his father, since he never lived at home after his admission to college. In his father's eyes employment by the Dowdeswell family was undoubtedly, in the Welsh phrase, a tidy job, offering both job security and the promise of support during retirement. In comparison life as a missionary combined high risk and low pay, as well as the explicit rejection of the family's traditional way of life. His two elder brothers seem to have taken the same view, and I was not aware of their existence until after my own time at university[6]. Owen did however maintain contact with his mother and younger sister Eva. Sadly none of his letters home survive.

Owen and Marjorie therefore experienced two very different childhoods. If there is a common factor it was the central importance of education as the road to self improvement. This would mould their thinking throughout life and prove crucial to the decisions that they took in the raising of their own children.

University and Work

After his admission to St Boniface College in 1924 Owen studied for entrance to university. He went up to Bristol University in 1926 in the same year as Marjorie where both studied history. They took their degrees in the summer of 1929 in the same finals examination. Owen must have received financial support from St Boniface to see him through his university education as his father was both unable and unwilling to support him in his choice of career. Marjorie's family would have well able to finance her studies.

There is little information about their three years at university although both worked hard for their degrees and it is clear from old photographs that Owen took a full part in college sports and that Marjorie was part of a lively social circle of female students. Family tradition is that Owen fell quickly for Marjorie's attractions but that she was much slower to see anything in him. Owen probably spent his vacations at St Boniface College to continue his historical and theological studies, while Marjorie returned to her family home in Gloucester. In August 1928 however, during their last summer vacation, they went on holiday together to Ogmore in South Wales where Owen wrote down two poems, possibly of his own composition. The final verses of the second poem read:

---

[6] Victor William James Griffiths died in 1976 in Wrexham. He appears to have married in Wrexham in the summer of 1930, but I have not checked the official certificate. Archibald Stephen Griffiths married Kathleen Ellen Tumath (born 4th June 1916) and they appear to have had 2 sons and a daughter. He died in 1978.

The sea is cruel and bitter, O God,
        Filled with the pain of the years;
        Its vast immense past human sense
Mocking at life's frail innocence
        Gives answer to human tears.

You spoke of the sea's great beauty,
        Giving peace of body and soul;
        Give me the grass and the trees that blow,
        God's sun above and the earth below,
        The surety that makes life whole.

The conversational tone of this piece suggests that Owen is responding directly to some comment by Marjorie on the beauty of the sea (ironical in the light of the separating seas of their later life). His response is that of the gardener wedded to the sun above and the earth below. Whatever their authorship they clearly meant a great deal to Marjorie, who kept the handwritten sheets till the end of her life. Both the writing and the retention of these poems strongly suggest that by this time, after 2 years on the same history course, Owen and Marjorie were committed to each other. It would however be another 6 years before they married.

Both were successful in obtaining their degrees. Despite an attack of the mumps Owen sat his examination and came away with a Second Class degree, Marjorie always believing that he would have obtained a First but for his illness. Marjorie also used her time at university to good effect. Another reference, dated 26th June 1929 from R Brown in the Department of History, praises her character and ability:

> Miss Vicker, I understand, is intending to apply for a Secretarial post. It is with great pleasure that I support such an application. Miss Vicker is an excellent student, careful and industrious. She has a good record in the University and has always done her work well. I feel perfectly confident that she has the gifts necessary for the work which she has chosen. She has an honours degree in History, and she is particularly well informed in current questions and in international affairs. She is pleasant to associate with, and she will, I am sure, carry out all her duties with the greatest care and zeal.

Little survives from the next three and a half years. After taking his degree Owen returned to St Boniface to complete his theological studies and his training for the ministry. He may by this time have moved out of the college, since he lived for some time in the small village of Horningsham, a few miles to the west of Warminster. He had a motor-cycle licence so that commuting between Horningsham and Warminster would have been easy enough. In one of the letters written after his liberation from internment he mentions Horningsham with affection and expresses the hope that he will have the opportunity to go there with Marjorie after his return to England.

On 21st December 1930 Owen was ordained deacon in Gloucester Cathedral by Bishop Arthur Cayley. The ceremony would have taken place in Worcester Cathedral but the Worcester see was temporarily vacant following the death of the previous bishop. The date remained an important anniversary for Owen throughout his life. After his ordination he took up his clerical duties in the parish of St Mary and All Saints, Kidderminster, where he worked for just over 2 years. In 1931, while living in this parish, he was ordained priest in Worcester Cathedral.

Knowing that her engagement would be a long one, and that she would need to wait until Owen had completed his training for the ministry and established himself with an income sufficient to support a family, Marjorie looked for clerical work. After leaving Bristol she undertook secretarial training, presumably in Gloucester, and then in April 1930 left home to take up a post at the head office of the Parents' National Education Union in Ambleside, in the heart of the Lake District. Her pay was £98 per year, rising to £100 in the second year. She spent two very happy years at Ambleside and photographs from that time show enjoying the grounds and surrounding countryside with colleagues of a similar age, and no doubt of a similar background and outlook. The aims and methods of the PNEU remained important to her throughout her later life as a wife and mother.

At Easter 1932 however she returned to her home in Gloucester to take care of her mother, Emily Mary, who was seriously ill. Marjorie, although determined to assert her independence in the matter of her marriage, felt that in other respects she was duty bound to support her family even at the cost of her personal interest. The nature of her mother's illness is unknown, but 10 years later, during the Second World War, she was again ill, this time suffering from lung cancer. She was however to live on until 1976 when she died at the age of 94. Marjorie's return home may have been an overreaction, as the family was well able to afford extra servants and nurses if those were needed. Her mother, who could at times be very demanding, may have insisted on Marjorie's return home. But possibly it was Marjorie herself who decided to throw up her rewarding job, perhaps to prove her family loyalty in spite of her marriage plans. Back in Gloucester Marjorie did manage to take some further temporary secretarial jobs in the period leading up to her departure for China in the autumn of 1934, but it is unlikely that these offered as much job satisfaction as she had experienced during her two years at Ambleside. She did however enjoy a cruise in the Mediterranean although a planned holiday in Germany was called off after Hitler's rise to power.

Throughout his youth Owen's aim had been to work as a missionary. Finally, on 19th January 1933 he embarked as a 2nd class passenger on the P&O ship SS Comorin in London docks for the long journey to Shanghai and on to Peking. There were 299 passengers on board, including at least 12 other missionaries bound for Hong Kong and Kobe. Owen's address on the passenger list is shown as Bridge House, Tewkesbury which suggest that he made a final visit to see his parents before travelling overseas. He would not have expected to return on furlough for at least 5 years. He was now fully embarked on the career that he had chosen some fifteen years previously. However both the pay and living conditions of missionaries in China made it very uncertain when, if at all, he would be able to invite Marjorie to share his life there.

CHAPTER 4

THE CHINA YEARS

Early Days

From Shanghai there were two main routes north to Peking. One option was to take a further ship north to the port of Tsientsin, and then the railway to Peking. The other option was to board a train at Shanghai and travel west via Nanking and Wuhan and then north to Peking. Whichever option Owen chose he probably arrived at his destination around the end of February 1933. Once there he took up residence in the Ch'ung Tê Boys School, attached to the Anglican Cathedral in the west of the city. The principal of the school was the Cambridge educated Dr Timothy Lin, who became a valuable mentor to Owen throughout his time in China and who took on the role of Bishop of North China after foreign clergy had left the country during the Second World War[7]. Owen no doubt made a full contribution to the work of the school, but the main purpose of his presence there was to enable him to learn sufficient Chinese to enable him to go out into the provinces and work as a missionary among ordinary Chinese people. In common with many other western missionaries he probably started his Chinese studies at the Peking Language School, and may well have met the American student George Kates who arrived there in June 1933. Kates was to immerse himself in the traditional Chinese life of Peking, and later wrote a classic memoir *The Years that Were Fat: Peking 1933-1940*, a description of life in Peking during the period that Marjorie and Owen lived there. Owen's assault on the Chinese language was a brave attempt, perhaps doomed to failure. Despite his obvious intelligence and determination Owen was never a linguist. While at St Boniface College he had been required to study one of the gospels in the original Greek. He had approached this task by memorising the entire gospel in the 1611 Authorised Version and managing to learn just enough Greek to identify where a passage for translation began and ended. In his examination he smoothly

---

[7] The author claims the unusual distinction of being possibly the only English boy to be named after a Chinese bishop.

translated the set passage, including in blissful ignorance the English text of two verses omitted from the Greek text put before him. This method was by no means new. In the account of his tour to the Lakes in 1797 an Oxford graduate J Grant wrote that "There have been instances of some of those candidates for orders getting the Greek of the four Gospels by rote, and the appropriate English for each verse, without understanding the language grammatically". At the age of 31 Owen was also a very late starter in Chinese, one of the languages most difficult for foreigners to master.

Quite apart from the challenge posed by the language, working as a missionary in China was neither safe nor comfortable. A posting to the Legation Quarter in Peking or to one of the foreign concessions in cities such as Tsientsin or Shanghai would ensure reasonable accommodation, a fair measure of security, and the support of fellow Europeans. Working in the provinces might involve almost total immersion in rural Chinese life and exposure to periodic outbreaks of anti-foreign sentiment. This could explode into murderous violence as in Tsientsin in 1870. This arose from allegations of the abduction and torture of children, and of gross sexual improprieties. When Henri Fontanier, the French consul, protested against the abuse and official inaction, and foolishly took aim at the provincial magistrate and killed a bystander, the local crowd took their revenge by murdering the consul and his aide, the 10 nuns in a Catholic convent, and 7 other French and Russian residents.

Thirty years later, during the Boxer uprising in 1899-1900, more than two hundred foreigners lost their lives, including forty four men, women and children who made up the missionary community of Shanxi province. The governor of the province had invited them to the provincial capital with a promise of safety and then ordered their execution. Another casualty was Baron von Ketteler, the Chief Minister of the German Legation in Peking. Perhaps forgetful of the fate of Henri Fontanier he had gone unarmed to protest at prevarication by the Zongli Yamen, the Chinese ministry for dealing with foreigners, but was murdered by a Boxer on his way there. His murder led to the siege of the foreign legations in Peking, an action led by the Boxers with overt support from the Empress Dowager Cixi. The siege was not lifted until Sikh troops of the British army finally broke through from Tsientsin on 13th August.

European governments inevitably reacted to these atrocities by making yet further demands on the Chinese governments, further ratcheting up the cycle of fear and distrust. One of the most visible manifestations of the new order was the construction of the much expanded and fortified Legation Quarter in the heart of China's capital city, looking north across Tiananmen Square to the Forbidden City, the historical seat of the Chinese imperial family. The new Legation Quarter was an entirely foreign enclave closed to all Chinese except those with official passes. As well as the British Legation, which occupied the largest area of all, it also contained in the 1930s the legations of Belgium, Denmark, France, Germany, Italy, Japan, the Netherlands, Portugal, Spain, and the USSR. There was also several major banks, a number of western shops and clubs, the luxury Grand Hotel des Wagons-Lits, and two hospitals (French and German). Peking's central railway station lay just outside the Tartar Wall to the south of the Quarter. Under the protocol established with the Chinese government in September 1901 foreign powers were allowed to retain up to 2100 troops in the Quarter as guards, together with around 30 heavy guns and 40 machine guns. To the south the Quarter was shielded by the old Tartar Wall, while substantial walls and a protective glacis were constructed to the west, north and east. The glacis was a broad open space used for drilling troops and for general recreation. Part of the glacis on the east side was set aside as a polo ground.

In the 1930s this was still recent history although, at least in Peking, the threat to European lives had diminished and most governments had reduced the number of troops stationed in the Legations. The main problem for the Chinese government was the steadily growing stranglehold exercised by Japan. China's defeat in the 1894 conflict had resulted in Japan acquiring control of Korea, Taiwan and Southern Manchuria. While the European powers were engaged elsewhere between 1914 and 1918 Japan seized areas of Shandong previously under German control and, following a series of provocations, had by 1933 established effective military influence over much of north east China, including Peking and the key city of Tsientsin and its port Tong King. The Chinese Nationalist government had moved to Nanking (southern capital), renaming Peking (northern capital) as Peiping (northern peace). The foreign legations maintained their presence in Peking, wary of exchanging their hard won security for new premises in Nanking where they would not have been able to establish a comparable Legation Quarter.

Owen's attempt to qualify himself to work as a missionary to the Chinese came to an unexpected end later in 1933 when the chaplain to the British Legation in Peking sailed home on furlough and made it clear that he did not intend to return to China. Owen was offered, and accepted, the temporary post of chaplain, and this subsequently became a permanent appointment. While he may have sensed some professional disappointment at this change of direction, his new job meant that he now had a guaranteed though modest stipend, comfortable accommodation, and sufficient assurance of personal security to allow him to propose that Marjorie should follow him to China and share his life.

Owen and Marjorie – Together in China, Part 1

We go back now to where we left Owen and Marjorie at the end of Chapter 1, on the point of their departure from their wedding tiffin. About fifteen miles to the west of Peking lies an area known as the Western Hills, famous for its groups of Buddhist temples. Writing in 1924 G E Hubbard describes their attraction for the expatriate community:

> Nearly a century ago the members of the Russian Mission, then and for long afterwards the only lay foreigners tolerated in Peking, hit on this little colony of temples as a retreat to flee to from the heat of the Peking summers. The earliest British Minister....followed their example when he established himself in Peking in 1860 and a series of his successors kept up the custom of renting temples at Pa-ta-ch'u [eight great places] for the hot season. Till the opening up of Peitaiho as a seaside resort accessible by railway, Pa-ta-ch'u continued to play the part of a small hill-station for foreigners, and even now the captivating beauty of the hills, with their brimming streams (after the breaking of the rains) and profusion of wild flowers, coupled with the cloistered charms of the temples themselves, rivals the cool waters of the Gulf of Chihli as a summer refuge for heat-worn residents in the capital.

Owen had probably had occasion to visit the area since his arrival in China in early 1933. After their exhausting journeys of the previous few days the short trip to the Western Hills would have seemed a far more attractive proposition than the six or seven hour train journey to the coast at a time of year when the weather was likely to be turning distinctly cold, if bright. At the conclusion of their wedding tiffin they would have been taken by the legation car to the foot of the hills where, as Hubbard notes, 'donkeys and carrying chairs are always waiting for hire at the terminus of the road'. From there it would have been a fair climb to Owen's chosen temple, described by Hubbard with Marjorie's underlining identifying the accommodation occupied on their honeymoon:

> One of the "Eight Places" was my home for a summer and thereby claims the first place on my list. It is seventh in order of altitude, standing over 500 feet above the plain, and is the largest, and probably the oldest, of the group, dating back historically to the 8th century, though, as often the case with Chinese monuments of great antiquity, the existing buildings are a comparatively modern replica of the original structures. Its name is Hsiang-chieh-ssu.
> We were tenants only of the topmost courtyard of all which we shared with the three priests who are the only modern representatives of a once flourishing community. On one side our neighbour was an ex-Minister of Finance who lived with his populous family in what was once the "Travelling Palace", on the other a diminutive wing of the temple thrown out over the valley with a marvellous view from its terrace had been converted to a week-end cottage by a compatriot man of business, while the various lower courtyards provided quarters for a considerable missionary population including a distinguished member of the body whom China had known for more than half a century.

A watercolour painting of the Bell Tower at the temple became a lifelong souvenir of their 9 night honeymoon in these rooms. After the stresses and strains of their lengthy engagement, and of the long journeys undertaken immediately prior to the wedding, the honeymoon was a chance to unwind and to renew their love for each other. Photographs show them both relaxed and happy, quite a contrast to the pictures of the wedding. And by the end of the honeymoon Marjorie may already have conceived her first child, John Richard born on 27th July 1935 just over 9 months later.

Owen and Marjorie returned from the Western Hills to their new home in Peking on Tuesday 22nd October. This would have been, at least initially, the Ch'ung Tê School, Jung Hsien Hutung, West City. I have been unable to establish for how long this remained their permanent home in China and when they took up residence within the British Legation compound.

There were frequent tensions within the expatriate community between missionaries and the diplomatic staff. While diplomats were trained to show sensitivity to the customs of the country, and on occasions developed a deep appreciation of Chinese civilisation, missionaries had a reputation for self-righteous tactlessness deriving from the perception that their job was to convert the Chinese from their heathen ways. As a result diplomats often found that they had the job of sorting out problems caused by the missionary community. This increased the existing Chinese suspicion that the missionaries acted as the vanguard of unwelcome and sometimes aggressive colonisation. Diplomats and missionaries tended therefore to move in different orbits, and Owen was perhaps unusual in having a firm foot in both camps. His work as chaplain to the Legation anchored him in the diplomatic community, but he and Marjorie retained their connections with the Anglican missions in Peking. He may well have been able to help in smoothing over any differences, at least at a local level.

There was quite a lively British community in Peking and Owen's work as chaplain would have included the normal routine of services in the chapel, and officiating at baptisms, marriages and burials. It is the normal duty of priests to comfort the dying and the bereaved but this duty, hard enough in itself, can at times require exceptional resilience and dedication. Owen faced such a challenge in January 1937 when Pamela Werner, a 17 year schoolgirl, was brutally murdered. Pamela was the daughter of E T C Werner, a former British consul who was a long-term resident in Peking and a writer about Chinese folklore. Having left her school in Tientsin, where she had brought to light sexual abuse by the headmaster, she was staying with her father in his home in the Tartar City, just outside the Legation Quarter. Her body was found near the Fox Tower, not far from her home. Her murderers had done their best to dispose of it completely, or at the least to make it unrecognisable. Her heart and other internal organs had been ripped out and, quite literally, thrown to the dogs. However it seems likely that the murderers had been disturbed as evidence left at the scene was sufficient to enable a positive identification of the body. Despite a joint investigation by the Chinese and British police no one was charged with Pamela's murder. Paul French, in his 2011 work *Midnight in Peking* points the finger of blame at the well-connected American dentist Wentworth Prentice and his friends. He also suggests, with much circumstantial evidence in support, that the British Legation and Foreign Office were complicit in obstructing the police investigation and that they consistently refused to take notice of further evidence gathered in the following years by Pamela's father, who pursued the case with a determination bordering on obsession. The suggestion of a cover-up is given added credence by the parallel refusal to take action against the Tientsin headmaster, who was allowed to return to England and to take up the post of secretary in a boys' school in Oxford. As with more recent accusations of institutional sexual abuse the authorities seem to have been more concerned to protect the abusers than the abused. A prime motive in the case of Pamela Werner would have been the imperative need to deflect suspicion away from the expatriate community and implicitly lay the blame on barbaric foreigners.

It is likely that Owen was fully aware of the dreadful mutilation of Pamela's body. Apart from anything else the British pathologist present at the autopsy was Dr William Graham Aspland, the man who had given Marjorie away at the wedding in October 1934. And, although Marjorie was by now half way through her second pregnancy, she too must have learned more than enough of the horrifying story through newspaper headlines and Legation Quarter gossip. As well as her friends within the diplomatic and missionary communities she had joined a circle of educated acquaintances centred on the University. Among her papers is a certificate of membership of the Peking Association of University Women (South Pacific Section) for the year 1940/41. I have no doubt that her membership dates back to her early years in China and enabled her to enjoy the conversation of an educated group as she had done at Bristol University and during her time at Ambleside. The difference now was that the Peking Association welcomed both Chinese and foreign members, and it is clear that Marjorie was able to form firm friendships with many of the westernised Chinese women who attended or worked at the University. For his part Owen enjoyed the opportunities for sporting relaxation within the foreign community. He played tennis and also hockey, and a photograph of the North China hockey team shows that this was composed exclusively of western males.

Michael Anthony, Owen and Marjorie's second son, was born in the German hospital in Peking on 21st May 1937. The hospital, staffed by German nursing sisters, was famous for its quiet and cleanliness as well as for the spiced cakes served with afternoon coffee. On occasions it served as a sanctuary for Chinese warlords who would rent a suite, bring their concubines, and perhaps enjoy their regular pipe of opium.

On Anthony's birth certificate Owen shows his address as the British Embassy in Peking, and it is possible that they were by this time living within the Legation Quarter. Anthony was baptised in the British Embassy Chapel on 13th June, with Owen officiating. Family tradition is that Marjorie was firmly expecting a daughter, to be called Margaret Anne, and that names corresponding to those initials had to be thought up quickly when the child turned out to be a boy. The elder son John always remained Marjorie's favourite, consolidating that position when in due course he married a girl called Margaret Anne. Anthony's birth in the German hospital was to cause him some problems in later life. Whereas John, born on British Legation premises, encountered no obstacles in his application to become a regular officer in the Royal Navy, Anthony met with considerable resistance from the Army when he tried to obtain a commission to serve as an officer in the school cadet corps at Newcastle Royal Grammar School. They appear to have suspected him, born in China in a German hospital, of being an enemy alien. The army cannot however have regretted their ultimate decision to approve his commission, and many years later recommended him for an MBE in consideration of his long service with the cadet force.

In summer Owen and Marjorie followed settled practice among the expatriate community in arranging a summer break in a bungalow at Peitaho. Peking is very cold in winter and brutally hot in summer. The winter cold can be countered by suitably thick clothing, like the traditional Chinese padded jackets and trousers, but there is little escape from the summer heat. Peitaho is a seaside town on the east coast of China, about 6 or 7 hours by train from Peking. Both diplomatic staff and missionaries were accustomed to holiday there, although strict social divisions were maintained. Wives and children would travel there in June, with husbands staying for some weeks in Peking to continue their work before joining their families in August. Peitaho, now usually transcribed as Beidahe, has retained its position as an upmarket seaside resort largely reserved for the senior hierarchy of the Communist Party.

Marjorie had arrived too late in the year in 1934 to enjoy this seaside break, and it is unclear whether they went to Peitaho in 1935. John's birth at the end of July may have come at an inconvenient time for any thoughts of a summer holiday. They would however have gone there in 1936 and, despite Anthony's birth on 21st May, they went ahead with their holiday plans in 1937. What followed next is best described in Marjorie's own words. This is the full text of a letter written on 4th March 1934 from Owen and Marjorie's temporary address – Guest House Flats, College Walk, Selly Oak, Birmingham 29:

> My dear Family,
> About 3 weeks ago I was overjoyed to receive this volume of letters and intended to do something about it immediately. But that was three weeks ago. It was grand to read of your doings for the past two years – but does anyone now possess the missing volumes 1934-36? I would very much like to see them.
> Well, now all about everything, as disgracefully I've scarce written a line to anyone since we arrived in November. We are here because it was necessary to earn our bread and butter somewhere for the space of a few months. Owen has a temporary appointment at St Mary's Selly Oak – January to July. We have a minute flat here – 1 living room which is chiefly nursery till 6.30pm; two beds; bath and tiny kitchenette. I'm trying hard to acclimatise myself to the domestic round again after such long abstinence – John and Anthony rather upset the regularity of the machine! Sometime in April I am going home again to spend 3 months with Mother before we sail, we hope. Owen's Mother will come to the flat for a time.
> Yes – we think we are going back, although the Bishop is still rather vague. In many ways we want to return – we feel that our

house is there – our furniture certainly is! – and we both love Peking and the Pekingese very much, tho' now of course things are very different & life will not be nearly so free & easy. We both of us rather dread leaving our parents again.

I'm not sure how much any of you, except René, know of our journeys. When Anthony was exactly a month old Owen conducted his family northwards and outwards to Peitaiho on the coast, and then abandoned us to our fate for the hot weather and returned to Peking. A month later things began to happen near Peking. Most of us at P.T.H. [Peitaiho] pooh-poohed the affair as the usual midsummer madness; there had been incidents about that time of year since the Japanese occupied Manchukou. The chief annoyance from my point of view was that there was no rail communication between P.T.H. and Peking, therefore no letters & no papers so we really didn't know what was happening. Every now and again stray letters came through when a train ran – but husbands said very little to alarm their wives! But we heard of the bombing of Tientsin; we saw dozens of bombers going over us daily, and we could hear the continual rumble of troop trains going south. Peking escaped – by arrangement, as it is presumably the future abode of Pu Yi[8] – but there were some ghastly scenes outside the city.

There came the time when we were told to be prepared to spend the winter in P.T.H. – temperature dropping to 20° below; no winter clothes; no heating in the houses; food already short & expensive. Some people who knew that they could not get back to their stations immediately began making preparations. Others with furloughs near made tracks for home. We were such ones. After a lot of argument Owen succeeded in insisting that I brought the boys home and he would follow after Christmas – he arranged as much as possible for us to go by boat to Shanghai and then P&O. Then came the bombardment of Shanghai – no boats with spare berths to Hong Kong for months – so I was to go to Japan. I think I would have passed out on my own in Japan! However the Bish said as we had 2 babes Owen had better come too & he elbowed his way up to P.T.H. to fetch us. He arrived on Saturday night & said that we were leaving at 3am on Monday - & we did. Eight & a half weeks later we reached England - & I think our journey in the early stages was characterised by our supposing "the worst is over now" only to

8 Pu Yi was the last child emperor, deposed in 1912 and later restored as a puppet ruler by the Japanese.

find more to come. The five hour train journey to the port of Tongkin took us over 20 hours in an overcrowded carriage thick with flies & dirt. We reached Tongkin at 1.30am to be told that owing to martial law we could not leave the station till 8am - & our ship was only 20 yards away! There was no waiting room so we sat on what luggage we had & fanned mosquitoes from the children (my legs have not been the same shape since) – we counted troop trains; tried to ignore a rowdy batch of Japanese troops – all amid mud, straw, manure, horses, guns & shell cases. At 6am Anthony wanted his early cup of tea - & as fortunately I was the cow it was all there. No sooner had we commenced operations than we were surrounded by a ring of enthusiastic Japanese & Annannese troops making encouraging noises, & no doubt bawdy comments.

At 8am we boarded the Navier Marci & believed the worst was over, we hadn't met the Japanese stewards. They made the lives of the English & Americans miserable for the next week. And of course we had to run into a typhoon, so instead of 4 days on the tub we were a week. I don't remember much about the typhoon except the noise as we were all too sick. Once there was an awful whack we heeled and shivered etc, but strange to say it did not sink. After the typhoon we steamed through the Inland Sea of Japan, which with Hong Kong harbour ranks as as one of the loveliest seascapes in the world. I'm not sure if it is worth a typhoon. It was again night when we reached Kobe with the storms etc, so Owen despatched us to the nearest hotel & stayed behind to repack. Weren't we glad to sleep in clean beds, have hot baths & a good breakfast – after the latter we moved our tents as the charges at that place were 30/- a night for one room & no food! We were 10 days in Kobe waiting for the Corfu & spent all our money. The little bits of old Japan we saw we loved – most of the young girls are exquisitely dainty; many wear European clothes, tho' most of them still wear the Kimono & obi with the odd & uncomfortable Japanese shoes. On wet days they wear wooden clogs brightly painted – the higher the more fashionable. The quieter streets are loud with the scuff-clip-clop as they walk along. But mostly Kobe is not quiet & we were nearly killed by motor cars after losing our motor sense in leisurely Peking where the motorist is always wrong & so has to be careful.

On Sept 21st we went on board the Corfu and had an uneventful tho' hot journey home. From Hong Kong we were laden with

Shanghai refugees including some 40 children. In Hong Kong harbour we saw the piled up carcases of five big liners which had gone aground in "our" typhoon – one being the Conte Verdi. Owen disembarked at Port Suez & motored through the desert to Cairo & visited the museum & saw the beautiful Tutankamen treasures – glimpsed the pyramids & recaught the boat at Port Said. We had a good view of Britain's might between Malta & Gibraltar. The ship opposite us in Marseilles was loading food supplies – she was bombed & sunk a few hours later. We had an escort until we reached the Bay of Biscay.

Since writing so optimistically about returning we have heard that the Embassy in Peking is practically deserted – all the working part is moving to Shanghai. We are now wondering if there will be anything to return to.

I enclose two snaps of the children. Sorry J's is so old – I can't find another at the moment.

Hoping to see most of you at Whitsuntide.

Much love, Marjorie

The brief historical background to this letter is that the Japanese had been steadily encroaching on Chinese territory for many years and had a generally peaceful, but intimidating, presence in Peking itself. While there had been numerous 'incidents' these had not resulted in open hostilities. However on 7th July 1937 an apparently minor flare up at the Marco Polo bridge 10 miles outside Peking escalated rapidly and became the starting point of the full scale Sino Japanese War which was to continue until VJ Day in 1945. By 20th July Japanese troops had encircled Peking, which they entered in triumph on 7th August, establishing their headquarters at the old Imperial Summer Palace. Meanwhile there had been massacres of both Chinese and Japanese garrisons at Tong Xian, a railway junction east of Peking on the line to Peitaho. On 13th August the Japanese began their assault on Shanghai, the start of a battle that lasted until the middle of November.

Owen and Marjorie's escape route was via Tongkin, the port of Tientsin. This involved travelling through territory now under Japanese control and Marjorie's passport contains an entrance visa dated 23rd August 1937. They were able to transit through Kobe, the final calling port for many P&O liners, as the UK and Japan were not then at war. Marjorie would come that way again in her later exit from

China in February 1941. While their voyage back from Kobe was largely uneventful Marjorie's reference to the bombing of the supply ship seen at Marseille is a reminder that the Spanish Civil War was also in progress in 1937. Presumably the ship was taking supplies to the Republicans and was sunk by the German bombers also involved in the attack on Guernica. Owen and Marjorie had truly fallen victim to the Chinese curse – may you live in interesting times! On arriving back in the UK they disembarked at Plymouth, travelling by train from there back to Cheltenham and Marjorie's family home in Gloucester.

The obviously uncomfortable sojourn in Selly Oak foreshadows some of the problems that they would encounter after the war. While Marjorie had no doubt helped her mother, and looked after herself at University and at Ambleside, she had never had to run a family without the help of servants. In China almost all the expatriate community employed one or several Chinese servants. Marjorie would have had the services at least of a cook and of an amah to look after the children. in Selly Oak she found herself trying to cope in very cramped conditions and without help. She was also cut off from her family and friends. Fortunately it was only for few months, as Owen was able to secure a new post as Director of Social and Religious Studies at the Peking Union Medical College, a prestigious university run by the Rockefeller Foundation. On 13th August 1938 Owen and Marjorie embarked on the Blue Funnel ship MS Patroclus bound from Liverpool to Shanghai. This time they were travelling first class, in a smaller ship with only 92 passengers in total.

Owen and Marjorie – Together in China, Part 2

On their return Owen retained his previous post as chaplain to the British Legation in Peking, in addition to his new post at PUMC. The duties at the British Legation were perhaps not onerous. As Marjorie made clear in her letter the bulk of the Legation staff had moved south, initially to Nanking and then, before the capture and sack of that city by the Japanese, to the new Nationalist capital at Chungking. It is however likely that Owen and Marjorie made their home in one of the houses or bungalows of the British Legation. There was now ample space, and living within the compound provided welcome additional security. In 1940 Mr Nikitin, who worked at the embassy of the USSR and had become a good friend, made a family film showing Owen playing with the children on the glacis surrounding the Legations. The film then goes to record a visit to a lake, probably the lake on the west side of the Forbidden City, and a ride in an Embassy car along Morrison Street with its trolleybus lines. Owen's scarf and Marjorie's fur coat indicate that the film was shot during the winter months, either at the beginning or end of the year.

Holidays in Peitaho continued despite the Japanese occupation of the whole of North China. There are some excellent photographs showing a relaxed and loving couple, and 2 children fully enjoying the seaside. Marjorie's membership of the Peking Association of University Women indicates that she was able to maintain many of her social contacts, even if much of the life had gone out of the Legation Quarter itself. In January 1941 she received as a leaving present a splendid album of Portrait Paintings by the contemporary Chinese artist Chiang Chao-Ho. This was given to her by 4 Chinese friends, Susan Wang, Han Hsueh-chien, Tien Chi-sheng and Pai Tuan.

Mention of a leaving present makes it clear that the China years were drawing to an end. The United Kingdom had declared war on Germany on 3rd September 1939. Japan, an ally of Germany, was not yet at war with the UK or the USA, but continued its offensive in China. Were Japan and the UK to enter into a state of war with each other then the position of Owen, Marjorie and the children would become very serious. In January 1941, after much agonising, Owen and Marjorie decided that Marjorie should travel to Canada with the children, leaving Owen to continue his work in China for as long as conditions permitted.

CHAPTER 5

LONG ROADS HOME

On 31st January 1941 Marjorie obtained a 14 day transit visa allowing her and the children to travel through Japan en route for Canada. She must have benefited from a short extension to this visa as it was only on 18th February that she obtained a USA transit certificate in Tientsin. On 15th February, when she received a short farewell letter and brushwork painting from another Chinese friend, she may still have been in Peking.

A label on Marjorie's old suitcase shows that she and the children sailed from Dairen on 21st February 1941 in State Room 4 on the Japanese ship Ussuri Maru of the Osaka Shosen K K shipping line. They may have taken a different ship for the short crossing of Liaodong Bay from Tientsin to Dairen. The passage on the Ussuri Maru took them from Dairen to Kobe, where they probably stayed in the Yamato Ryokan Hotel. The Ussuri Maru, built in 1932, subsequently became one of the 'hell ships' used for transporting Japanese prisoners of war. It was sunk on 28th June 1944 in an American air strike while on a voyage out of Manila. In Kobe they transferred to Cabin 219 on the SS President Coolidge bound for San Francisco. This ship, launched in 1931 as a luxurious Pacific liner, was used in 1941 by the US War Department for civilian evacuations and later as a transport ship for reinforcing garrisons in the Pacific. In October 1942 it struck 2 mines laid by the American Navy to protect the harbour in Vanuatu and has since become a major attraction for undersea divers.

Marjorie and the children disembarked in San Francisco on 13th March.. On the following day they arrived at White Rock in British Columbia and were granted a 1 year visa by Canadian immigration. A year later this permit would be renewed 'for the duration of the war'. Their initial residence in Canada was at 3298 Lonsdale Avenue, North Vancouver. Later, certainly by 1943, they moved to Queens Road West in the same area across the bay from the city centre.

When Marjorie sailed from Tientsin in 1941 she could not in her worst nightmares have imagined that this would be the start of a separation that would last for more than 4 years. The plan was that Owen would remain in China for as long as it seemed safe for him to do so, and then sail across the Pacific to rejoin his family. For the time being he continued to live in the bungalow within the British Legation compound in Peking, although most of the furniture had been crated and shipped out of China. It would eventually come to England and take its place in the various homes that they occupied from 1945 onwards.

It is unclear what news, if any, Marjorie received from Owen in the period from March to September 1941. Right up to the end of her life she kept a box which contains Owen's few communications from internment and his complete letters from the weeks after his liberation in February 1945. There is however nothing from him dated earlier than October 1941. She was clearly worried enough to write to their friend and fellow missionary David Paton to ask what news he might have. David Paton replied on 14th September, writing from Mount Omei, a Chinese sacred mountain near Chengtu in Szechuan, where he was involved in a three week conference:

> Thank you very much for your letter, which was there to welcome me when I got Chungking, about three or four weeks ago.
> I have been thinking about you all a good deal, since the freezing of credits & so on – there is no news from North China, & I have no letters myself, all my stuff being held up in Chungking: but I have seen a letter from [name unclear] & another from Owen, both to Y T Luo, of the end of July, so I was relieved, as the situation "broke" earlier than that. Owen personally will be glad that he got you out of the way: & you will be acquiring grey hairs worrying about him.

The reference in this letter to the situation having broken in the summer of 1941 probably refers to the serious outbreak of fighting between Chinese and Japanese forces in the area between the Yellow River and the Yangtze. The Japanese gained the upper hand in these battles, partly, no doubt, because, in a continuation of the internal civil war, the Chinese Nationalists under Chiang Kai-Shek had previously put out of action the highly effective Communist 4th Route Army. A month after hearing from David Paton Marjorie received what may have been her first message from Owen. On 12th October, the day before the 7th anniversary of their marriage, Owen sent a telegram with the short message, “Genesis twenty nine twenty”. This refers to the verse in the Bible which says, “And Jacob served seven years for Rachel; and they seemed with him but a few days, for the love he bare to her.”. That the telegram was correctly addressed to Marjorie at 3298 Lonsdale Avenue indicates that Owen had at least received accurate information of her whereabouts.

This was followed by 3 further telegrams. On 17th October Owen cabled, “Sailing from Tientsin November Seventeen.” On 8th December he continued, “In Manila Great Eastern Hotel. Expect long delay. Possibility temporary work here. No money difficulty yet.” And on 23rd December, “Christmas love darlings Bunny John Anthony. Fairly quiet here. Little danger. Comfortable home.” And after that, again the silence.

These messages and silences need to be read in the context of the developing and worsening international situation. The Japanese army occupied Peking in 1937 and was still there in 1941. As noted above military advances by the Japanese led in that year to a significant deterioration in the position, with probable additional risk to foreign nationals then in the large area of China controlled by Japan. Japan was not however then at war with the United Kingdom. That came about on 7th December with the attack on Pearl Harbour, and on the same day (8th December in the Philippines) the Japanese air force began bombing Manila. On 23rd December Owen would still have been living in freedom in Manila, although the Japanese had invaded the Philippine islands and would enter the city on 2nd January 1942. From the evidence of the article quoted below we know that Owen had taken a temporary post under Bishop Binsted of the Protestant Episcopal Church at the cathedral in Manila. This was not of course his original intention, since he had paid $400 for the passage from Tientsin to San Francisco, with the intention of rejoining Marjorie and their sons in Canada, but had been unable to proceed further than Manila.

On Sunday 4th January American and British residents were ordered to report to specified places of registration. A first group of 300 residents were interned at Santo Tomas, the university campus in Manila. By 14th January the camp held 3100 internees: 2000 in the main building,

400 in the annex, and 700 in the gymnasium. Owen, on his move into the camp on 6th January, was allocated a space in the gymnasium.

For some weeks there was hope that the Japanese occupation would prove to be temporary. The Americans under General MacArthur continued to hold out on the island of Corregidor but eventually were forced to withdraw. It would be 3 years before they were able to return. For several months Marjorie received no news, being left completely in the dark as to whether Owen was alive and, if so, where he was being held. She wrote again to David Paton, who replied from Chungking on 16th April:

> I had better come to the point at once, and say that there is virtually no news here about Manila, except that things seem to be not too bad. If there was anything like Hongkong going on, I think we should have heard – probably through MacArthur. And we have not heard of anything much of that kind. So I think you can probably assume that Owen is safe, though you may not get any more news for some time. I said more or less this in a mailbag letter I sent off about a fortnight ago, and I delayed this while I asked around in the Press Hotel and other such places – but without success.
>
> I am afraid it is just beastly for you: and I wish I could produce some good news. But I can't. You probably know the kind of situation that is prevailing in the various places. In Peking, Tientsin and Shanghai (and other places in occupied China), foreigners are allowed so much money and normally allowed to keep their homes, and they make do, living retired-like and eating rather less than usual. In Hongkong when the worst was over, they were all herded off into camps, where they are given two bowls of rice a day and a very little vegetables. If they have Chinese friends extra stuff can be brought into them. Many of them will surely die if this goes on indefinitely. (The Japanese are always worst when they have to fight for a place, or where it stands as a hated symbol. Hongkong qualified under both heads.) Manila they didn't have to fight for: they probably won't have such a relatively nice time as they had in Shanghai (the foreigners I mean); but I don't think it can be anything like Hongkong..........

> Heaven knows when this will get through to you. Letters are being impossibly slow, I think because there are too many of them for the censors in India or for the planes or something. ....
> I am afraid there is nothing very consoling for you in all this – I wish there was. I shall look forward a lot to getting the letter you cabled about. And I will write and send a mailbag message if I do get anything.

In the meantime Marjorie had clearly tried to obtain information from the UK Foreign Office, presumably by writing to A L Scott who had worked at the Legation in Peking in the pre-war years. Foreign Office envelopes postmarked 1st February and 7th April 1942 evidence that she received replies but neither side of the correspondence has survived. Finally, however, Marjorie received news direct from Owen, in an undated letter. On internal evidence this was probably written after several months of internment:

> I am kindly allowed to write a note to you. Living with Rev. Spackman in internment camp as voluntary internees for religious work. I am very well and there is much interesting work to do. Thinking of you three always and trying to share your life. We have enough food, and extras can be obtained from stores and vendors inside. No shortage of tobacco of sorts. Lots of men like myself longing to rejoin our families but no despondency. Courage, dear heart – I hope the lads are well and helping you – cannot speak of my longing for you, it is too great for words. Later we will make up for all these empty months. A big hug each for John and Anthony and much love. For you, all the love and longing in the world. Hope you can last out financially till I come – there will be no difficulty then. Threefold love darling Bun. Teddy.

This was the only letter that Owen was able to send to Marjorie during his 3 years of internment and, like the very few later telegrams, was subject to Japanese censorship. What he may have recounted to Marjorie after the war remained between them. He did not discuss his experiences with others.

Disbelief might well be one's initial reaction to Owen's statement that he and Rev Spackman were *voluntary internees for religious work*. After all they had been rounded up with all other foreign nationals in the first week of January 1942 and transferred to the Santo Tomas compound. However an article which Owen wrote after his release confirms that it was his decision to stay in Santo Tomas, and also provides much useful information about his life and work there. It was drafted in March and April 1945, while he was awaiting repatriation from the Philippines, and published in the September 1945 issue of *Forth*, the official newsletter of the Protestant Episcopal Church of America.:

The Church Carries On in Santo Tomas
Limited Camp Life Developed Real Fellowship
By the Rev O A Griffiths

(A rector of the Church of England, Mr Griffiths was caught in the Philippines by the outbreak of the war. Until his internment he was an assistant at the Cathedral of St Mary and St John, Manila. When missionaries were allowed to resume their tasks in 1942, he chose to stay at Santo Tomas to share the experiences of prison life about which he writes.)

On the evening of the Festival of the Epiphany, 1942, a group of Episcopalians was gathered together in the compound of the Cathedral of St Mary and St John, Manila, when a Japanese officer appeared and ordered us to be ready to leave within half an hour for the Santo Tomas Internment Camp. Instructions were given to take enough food for four or five days. Not five days but more than three years later on February 23, 1945, the majority of this group were released from Los Baños by a daring and brilliantly executed combined move by MacArthur's paratroopers, amphibian tank corps, and Filipino guerillas. Those two dates mark the beginning and end of a period not only of discomforts and privations but also of unique opportunities for carrying on our work.

The group, cramming necessities into their suitcases on that fateful January 6, comprised all the Church's missionaries in Manila, with the exception of Bishop Norman S Binsted who was held at the High Commissioner's House where he had been giving his services as interpreter and liaison officer; Bishop Robert F Wilner who was visiting the missions in the Mountain Province and who was subsequently interned at Baguio; and two or three others who had already been picked up and were temporarily interned in Villamoor Hall.

We proceeded to the University of Santo Tomas where all "aliens" were being taken, crowding the rooms, patios, and grounds.

The first few days in Santo Tomas presented a picture of almost complete chaos. There was no semblance of life in community. But gradually more order began to appear as people settled down to their new life and in time the camp became a community with a well-organized life. It must be remembered that the Japanese did nothing for us except to provide sleeping quarters and questionnaires! No beds or bedding, no food, no adequate water supply or toilet facilities, no hospital, kitchen, or laundry services. The internees had to build up all the essential services of a normal town with a population of nearly four thousand, and organize squads of men and women for the smooth running of these services.

On the first Sunday in camp we celebrated the Holy Communion; the paten was a saucer and the chalice a cheese glass, and the service was conducted in the midst of a crowd of people scurrying to and fro preparing their breakfast and amid the rumble of garbage cans. But the service was held and despite all difficulties and changes we were able to hold that service every Sunday at least throughout the whole period of internment.

Ten days after internment a change took place which altered the whole direction of the religious life of the camp. The Japanese authorities gave permission to all missionaries to return to their homes and work. This inevitably raised the question as to the best way of serving the needs both of those on the outside and those in camp. I volunteered to stay in camp to serve the needs of the internees. I was temporarily unattached and, being a transient, was not closely in touch with the work on the outside.

Those who went outside to resume their regular work were of untold help to the religious life of the camp, upholding me by their prayers and supplying me with religious necessities, books, and food.

The religious committee of the camp represented many different denomination viewpoints but despite divergent backgrounds of Church order, doctrine, and worship we worked together "with one accord" and maintained the "unity of the Spirit" throughout the years. All would be agreed that one of the happiest and deepest of our experiences during internment was the spiritual and mental fellowship which we shared.

The work developed along usual lines: full Sunday services, a midweek service, and daily morning prayers; Sunday School and Young People's groups; general discussion groups and lectures. What was unusual was the environment and the amount of interest aroused among many who had formerly been opposed or indifferent. One of the most valuable features of the work were the various series of lectures. Internment is not a desirable experience for anyone but it did give large numbers of men and women the opportunity to do much more reading and thinking than they had done before, and many of them began to be much more concerned about the international situation.

Two series of lectures, especially, aroused keen interest. The first, entitled The Shape of Things to Come, was, as the Wellesian name implies, an attempt to work out something in the nature of a blueprint for the postwar world. A large number of internees, bankers, economists, lawyers, businessmen of all kinds, engineers, educators, and ministers of religion, were divided up into groups each of which was responsible for the examination of a particular subject. The findings of each group were submitted at combined meetings of all the groups, and after full discussion and revision, the report was presented at a large public meeting. As I recall the accumulated findings and the general picture that resulted I cannot shake off the very curious, *albeit* absurd, feeling that many delegates who took part in the Dumbarton Oaks Conference must somehow have been present in Santo Tomas in the fall of 1942!

The second series requires an explanation of the background against which it was given. During internment ministers of religion were brought into the closest possible contact with "all sorts and conditions of men". How close that contact was will be understood more readily when it is stated that during the early days of internment in Santo Tomas well over seven hundred men were housed in the gymnasium. Each man occupied a living space of twenty-four square feet and there were six toilets for the whole group. Within that space one slept and kept all one's personal belongings. Almost literally "cheek by jowl" men of all kinds, good and bad, learned and ignorant, rich and poor, lived their lives day after day, week after week, through what seemed interminable years. This state of affairs tended very quickly to the breaking down of many of the barriers existing in normal life and created an atmosphere in which both questions and criticisms were freely aired. The most frequent concerned the disunity of Christendom, a matter which nearly all laymen viewed with considerable impatience. They confirmed my own opinion that the divisions of the Church are a greater "scandal" to the so-called "man-in-the-street" than they are to large numbers of regular Churchgoers who seem to regard our degrees of separateness as part of the established order of things. Other questions revealed almost complete ignorance of what the Church is thinking, saying, and doing about the vast problems with which we are confronted today.

Out of such a situation came a series of lectures on the Oxford and Edinburgh Conferences which gave to many a measure of enlightenment and encouragement. They came to see that the Christian Church with the profound insights engendered by its faith is interpreting that faith boldly and relevantly in terms of the political and economic life of the world. Furthermore, they came to have a fuller and more sympathetic understanding of the difficulties which must be overcome before complete unity can be achieved.

On May 14, 1943, eight hundred men were transferred from Santo Tomas to Los Baños to prepare a new camp. I chose to go with this group but before leaving sent an SOS to Bishop Binsted on behalf of the people in Santo Tomas who would be left without the ministrations of the Church. Soon after we had arrived at Los Baños the news came that the Rev B H Harvey had entered Santo Tomas. All was well.

Our life and work at Los Baños followed along much the same lines as at Santo Tomas. And here, in July 1944, practically all the members of the Episcopal group were reunited, the Japanese military authorities having decided to re-intern all religious workers. They came just in time to share all our worst experiences; but despite the serious deficiency of food with consequent physical and mental weakness, the full services of the Church were carried on. Despite all difficulties with which we were "sore let and hindered" the Church carried on.

There are 3 other main sources for Owen's time in internment:

1. An American journalist, A V H Hartendorp, was appointed as camp historian by the (mainly) American organising committee. Working in secret, and in the knowledge that discovery of his work would lead to his being executed, he compiled a daily typescript diary. *The Santo Tomas Story*,

published in 1964, is an abbreviated version of this diary, edited so as to provide a continuous narrative. It is invaluable in providing an overall history of the camp but, perhaps inevitably, focuses mainly on the manifold and difficult challenges faced by the organising committee in their work of running the camp. Like Owen's article above it also deals mainly with Santo Tomas, with relatively little material about the satellite camp in Los Baňos where Owen spent the greater part of his time in internment.

2. A formal statement, typed by Owen after his return to England, which deals with the execution of 3 escapees in February 1942. I once read this statement, and can confirm that Owen's statement is in line with Hartendorp's account of this incident.
3. A series of letters, the Liberation Letters (abbreviated LL), written by Owen to Marjorie after his liberation, but while he was still in the Philippines awaiting repatriation to England.

In the article quoted above Owen clearly explains the reason for his choosing to accept voluntary internment in Santo Tomas. But he may soon have regretted this decision. On 11th February 3 internees, 2 English and 1 Australian, escaped from the camp. They were recaptured on the following days and severely beaten. Despite initial assurances to the contrary they were then court-martialled and condemned to death. The executions were carried out on Sunday 15th February. Owen responded to the request of the camp commandant, Lieutenant Tomayasu, for a minister to accompany the three men to the place of execution, on the clear understanding that he would not be required to witness their deaths. According to Hartendorp's account he offered the men what religious consolation he could and promised that, on his own eventual return to England, he would convey any messages that they wished to send to their families. According to his own account, in the typescript copy of a formal statement made after the War, he was asked by Lieutenant Tomayasu to inform the men of the justice of their sentence but, disregarding this instruction, he made it clear that their execution was in clear contravention of the rules for the treatment of prisoners and that he would make a full report to this effect on his return to England. It was no doubt fortunate for him that Lieutenant Tomayasu did not understand English. The men were then taken a short distance away, ordered to sit on the edge of a freshly dug trench, and shot several times before their bodies were covered with earth by Filipino cemetery workers. Owen then came to the graveside and read the Church of England service for the dead, with the Japanese officers and soldiers standing respectfully in the 'salute' position. The article in Wikipedia listing all war crimes makes no mention of this incident, so that it is likely that Owen's draft affidavit did not result in any prosecution. When one notes that there were similarly no prosecutions in respect of the infamous Burma railway this should perhaps cause us no surprise.

Religious services had started in the camp on 11th January, the first Sunday after the initial transfer of internees into the camp. These became a regular feature of Owen's life over the next 3 years. He was to tell Marjorie that "in every place we have been we have managed to hold that service [Holy Communion], sometimes in incredibly awkward & noisy places but no Sunday of internment has gone by without a celebration". And again: "in the crowded life of internment & here [i.e. in the temporary post-liberation camp] it has never once been possible to hold a service where one was freed from the noises of bustling activity in the immediate vicinity". According to Hartendorp the number of internees attending religious services was no more than 150 to 200, a small minority of the total camp population. The influence of Owen and other ministers of religion on the life of the camp may well however have extended well beyond this core group of regular attendees at the Sunday services.

Santo Tomas was a mixed community, with men, women, children, and family groups. In addition to regular weekly services Owen therefore officiated at the accustomed services for baptisms, marriages and funerals, although the Japanese authorities did their best to discourage both marriages and pregnancies[9]. Owen mentions the baptism in 1942 of the son of Jim McGregor, an employee of the Hongkong Shanghai Bank. And in 1963, on the annual summer visit for Speech Day at St John's School in Leatherhead, he had a totally unexpected meeting with Mr & Mrs Haines, whose marriage he had performed when they were in internment. Fortunately there were no

[9] Hartendorp reports the reproof given by a Japanese officer to one of the men concerned: "Don't you know the Military do not permit interned persons to engage in the business of making babies?"

further attempts at escape; the internees recognised that there was no prospect of Europeans disappearing into the local Filipino community, and absolutely no hope of getting off the islands to American-controlled territory. Uncomfortable living conditions and inadequate nutrition did however result in an increased death rate.

Owen was perhaps fortunate in that he had work to do, and a clearly defined position in the camp community. Most internees were completely cut off from their previous occupations, and inevitably boredom was a major problem, however hard the camp committee and the internees worked to provide amusements and other activities. Owen' status in the camp is underlined by the fact that he allowed himself to be nominated as a candidate in elections held in January 1943 for a new executive committee. Owen obtained 67 votes, being placed 4th out of 6 candidates in the British section. He would not therefore have secured a place on the committee, but in any case the Japanese authorities refused to acknowledge this exercise in democracy and appointed their own nominees.

Lectures and other Diversions

Hartendorp reports an audience of around 2000 for the monthly variety shows, and adds that almost the whole population of the camp would turn out for the rare treat of a movie and listen to the regular evening music broadcasts. That Owen does not mention these entertainments in his article and letters does not mean that he did not attend the shows or listen to the music, but he probably did not consider them to be important. In his later life he never showed any interest in music or films. A hint may be found in one of his letters where he mentions the nightly open-air cinema provided by the Americans after liberation, "but my favourite form of entertainment still runs along internment lines – sitting with a group of friends round a fire, smoking and drinking coffee". He obviously did take a very active part in the political and religious lectures and discussions mentioned in his article, and in the Liberation Letters he comments frequently on his attempts to catch up with the international political situation after his years in internment when he received no news of what was happening in the outside world.

He was himself responsible for another series of lectures not mentioned in the article. In one of his letters he writes to Marjorie:

> You may probably have heard from some repatriated folk in the past that my contribution to the educational programme in the camp was a most brilliant! series of lectures on English Literature. For myself it was a great joy to make as thorough a study as resources in books allowed of a subject concerning which my specific knowledge was hazy and now I am quite a devotee – nearly all of my non-theological reading being confined to books on or about literature in addition to the English classics. We were very short of material but I managed to write nearly 70 lectures covering the period from "Beowulf" to Masefield: but alas! they are all lost & two years or more of hard work has gone up in smoke. But what a nice mental life it gave me & a subject of the most absorbing interest.

Owen's lectures clearly started when he was still at Santo Tomas. It is less clear whether they were completed there, or whether he continued this series of talks after his transfer to Los Baños on 14th May 1943. This transfer would have resulted in the loss of much of his previous audience, and his ability to research the subject had presumably relied on the university library on the Santo Tomas complex. On the other hand Owen refers in the letter quoted above to two years or more of hard work, and it seems unlikely, assuming a weekly lecture, that he would have completed his talks in the 16 month period between his original internment and the transfer to the new camp.

Communications and Marjorie's Return to England

In the days immediately after his transfer to Los Baños Marjorie received what may have been her first communication since his initial letter referring to his status as a voluntary internee. This was a telegram sent from Philippines Internment Camp No.2, in which he describes his health as 'good' (could it have been anything else in a message subject to censorship?) and writes:

> Special love to Anthony this month. Names of Canadians and those having dependents [sic] in Canada asked for. Mine has been given. Threefold love and longing.

As Anthony's birthday was in May this enables us to date this telegram with some precision. Marjorie again contacted the Foreign Office, sending a telegram to A L Scott on 5th July, and received the following reply, dated 21st July, from G A Wallinger of the Prisoners of War Department:

> Mr A.L. Scott has discussed with me, as the member of the Foreign Office who is most directly concerned with the projected exchange of civilians with Japan, your telegram of 5th July. He is kindly enclosing this personal line in a letter of his own.
>
> We have not put forward your husband's name for repatriation on this occasion; and, since he has a good claim for consideration, I think I owe you some explanation of this decision.
>
> Let me first take the general considerations: they are that we are concentrating our efforts, so far as the United Kingdom is concerned – and I add this because the same does not apply for instance to Australia – on releasing from Japanese hands all who have been imprisoned by the Japanese gendarmerie, all children who are separated from their parents, mothers with young children and the seriously sick. We are not going to be able to release all of these persons and indeed anything like all of them, for out of a possible total of some 12,000 British subjects in Japan, Manchuria, occupied China, Indo-China, Siam and the Philippines, even if all goes according to plan, only some 600 are to be repatriated.
>
> Turning now to the particular case of your husband, what has most influenced our decision not to put forward his name has been the fact that we have information that his ministrations to his fellows in adversity have been of the greatest help to them and that his departure would leave them with an irreplaceable void. There will be many hundreds of British subjects left after the repatriation, in the camp in which he is working, and we have taken their welfare and spiritual comfort into consideration in reaching our decision. Had the Swiss been represented in the Philippines, we would have given Mr Griffiths himself the opportunity of making a choice; but in the absence of any neutral representative, we have had to make the decision here. From what I have heard of him, I believe he would say that our decision has been the right one.
>
> I know that this letter can be but cold comfort to you: but I have written personally and fully so that you may know that we have looked into the case of your husband fully and conscientiously; and

I hope that you will be able to find some solace in the consciousness that it is owing to his qualities and capacity for service to others that his own claims have, on this occasion, been overridden.

This letter is further evidence of Owen's valuable work in the camp. One may however doubt that he would have approved of the decision taken in his case. The May telegram is a clear expression of hope that he might be included in the list for repatriation. Negotiations on the list of those to be repatriated must have dragged on for some time. One of his letters indicates that 2 of his acquaintances in the camp reached Vancouver on M/S Gripsholm in early December 1943, both having promised to pass on news to Marjorie. M/S Gripsholm, built in 1924 by Armstrong Whitworth at Newcastle-upon-Tyne, was the world's first transatlantic liner with diesel engines. Between 1942 and 1946 she was chartered by the US Department of State and, sailing with a Swedish crew under the flag of the International Red Cross, made 12 round-trips and repatriated over 27,000 prisoners in exchanges with the Germans and Japanese.

In the first six months of 1943 Owen was able to transmit at least 2 other messages to Marjorie. A further undated telegram may have been sent from Manila:

> 1942 letters received with great delight. Thinking of you always. Deepest love to you three and Mother. Need, when possible, brown shoes (sevens), blades, tobacco.

And on 27th May 1943 a radio message was picked up by Gerard Motors (dealers in Dodge and Plymouth cars and trucks).

> The following is a report of a short wave broadcast received direct from radio station JLG-4, Tokyo, Japan, on May 27, 1943, at 6.20pm Central War Time. This broadcast was on a frequency of 15,105 megacycles. Every day at this time the Tokyo radio broadcasts messages from American prisoners of war. This message was read by the station announcer and is as follows:
> From: Reverend O Andrew Griffiths, Age 41, interned at Santo Tomas University, Manila, Philippines

To: Rockefeller Foundation, 49 West, 29th Street, New York, New York
Message: Will you kindly convey the following message to my wife: - My dear, I am a voluntary internee in the camp in Manila, helping in various ways by services and lectures. I am very well – bodily well cared for, good food and clothes. You precious three are in my thoughts continually. [few words lost here while changing records] – Your inquiry of January reached me in September. So long a delay. Courage, dear heart, for the sake of the future. My love to you ________, and John and Andrew and to my mother. With deep thanks to the Rockefeller Foundation from Rev O A Griffiths of the CUNC. Signed O Andrew Griffiths
Receiving conditions were fairly good here today and you may have a copy of the master record if you wish. Please refer to the date of the broadcast and to Master Record No 203 and 204.
Yours very truly [signed] R P Read

This broadcast was recorded live onto a 7 inch 78rpm disc, with some words being lost in mid-message when the disc was turned over to capture the end of the message. Marjorie's box of papers contains both the master record and the original typed transcript on the headed notepaper of Gerard Motors, 701-703 Excelsior Avenue, Hopkins, Minnesota (telephone Hopkins 7614-5). In addition to the gap in the message there are some obvious transcription errors, particularly *Andrew* for both *Ambrose* and *Anthony*, and *CUNC* for *PUMC*. Evidence of Japanese censorship is strong in Owen's assurance the he is "bodily well cared for, good food and clothes", and also in the fact that such messages were read by a Japanese announcer to ensure that the POW or internee had no opportunity to depart from the censored script during a live broadcast. Nevertheless Marjorie must have been relieved that receiving conditions on that evening were sufficiently good to enable her to receive an intelligible message.

We do not know when Owen submitted the message to Japanese radio. On internal evidence however there can be little doubt that he did so when we was still at Santo Tomas camp in Manila, therefore at some time between October 1942 and April 1943. Communication between internees and their families was, to put it mildly, never a priority with the Japanese authorities. This message is evidence that an inquiry sent by Marjorie in January 1942, presumably seeking information on his whereabouts, did not reach him until September of that year. No wonder therefore that Marjorie had tried to obtain information from David Paton and from the Foreign Office.

Only 2 other telegrams reached Marjorie. The first is dated 22nd June 1944 in which Owen, after the customary reassurance that he is in good health, writes:

> Am well, receiving letters and cards. Deep love to you, John, and Anthony always. Waiting with all the patience I have! Love to both Mothers.

And finally an undated telegram:

> No questioning your possible Spring move: it is our ultimate destination anyway. Lads' school progress most satisfying. Life filled with love, longings, work. Your Teddy.

This second telegram was sent to Vancouver and is date-stamped 28th March 1945 by the Post Office in North Lonsdale before being forwarded to 43 Heathville Road, Gloucester, England. By the end of March 1945 Owen had been writing daily letters for nearly 5 weeks in the period following his liberation from internment. The most probable explanation is that this telegram was sent to Canada in March 1944, and that the Post Office in Vancouver made a mistake with the postmark. Notes left by John suggest that Marjorie and the children left Vancouver on Monday 27th March, in which case the telegram from Owen arrived on the day after their departure. The fact that Owen sent a further telegram to Canada 3 months later is evidence that he had not by then received confirmation of Marjorie's return to England.

Marjorie's 3 years in Canada came to an end in April 1944. There is little evidence for that period, although we know that John and Anthony both had whooping cough, attended the local school in the road where they lived in North Lonsdale, and enjoyed playing in the stream which crossed the road a couple of hundred yards beyond the school. This road now leads to the cable car used by tourists for the ride up Grouse Mountain. Marjorie no doubt had her hands full in coping by herself with the 2 young boys, and in making ends meet on a limited income. Owen's decision, made back in 1938, to take employment with the Rockefeller Foundation at Peking University Medical College had the fortunate consequence that the Foundation was willing to provide financial support to Marjorie during this long period of separation. It is unclear whether her family in England were able to send her any other financial assistance during these war years. Owen's letter 20 refers to the help that Marjorie received in her early Canada days from a Mrs Handsmith but, as far as I can recall, Marjorie made no permanent friends in Canada. Throughout her life she was diligent in maintaining contact with members of her family and with friends she had made in China, but there were no exchanges of letters with those whom she had known in Vancouver.

Marjorie would no doubt have waited in Canada for Owen's liberation and return. However in 1943 her father had a colostomy and was diagnosed with terminal cancer of the colon. No doubt making use again of her contacts with the Foreign Office Marjorie was now successful in obtaining permission to return to England to see her parents again, and on Monday 27th March she and the 2 boys took the long train journey across the continent from Vancouver to Halifax, arriving there on Saturday 1st April. On the following Monday they boarded the MS Cavina, and sailed on 7th April with 20 other merchant ships to join convoy HX 286 which had departed from New York 2 days earlier. There were altogether 88 merchant ships in the combined convoy, with an escort of 5 or 6 ships from the Royal Navy, the B.VI Escort Group. MS Cavina was a Fyffes refrigerated banana boat, on this occasion carrying a cargo of general meats. According to Marjorie's recollections the other passengers were a woman travelling with her daughter, an airforce widow with 2 children, a governess accompanying the daughter of the Consul General in Shanghai, and an unspecified number of Canadian army officers. All passengers were told that the ship would not stop for any emergency, and Marjorie had a period of severe panic when John went missing. She feared that he had fallen overboard, but eventually found him chatting to the stokers in the engine room. At one point severe weather caused the convoy to scatter, but no ships were lost and MS Cavina, originally bound for Liverpool, arrived at Loch Ewe on Friday 21st April. It then sailed around the north of Scotland and docked at Leith on Sunday 23rd April. Marjorie and the children disembarked and took the train from Edinburgh to Gloucester.

Marjorie did arrive home in time to spend some weeks with her father before his death on 30th August 1944 at the age of 68. She was also able to arrange for John and Anthony to resume their education at the King's School in Gloucester, pending Owen's return and a decision on where they would then live and work. None of this became known to Owen until after his liberation. Since his telegram dated 22nd June 1944 was sent to Canada it is clear that he was not then aware that Marjorie's proposed Spring move had become a reality. While this telegram confirms that he was receiving letters and cards, these must have been posted before Marjorie's return to England, indeed before she had made any definite arrangements for this return. He may have received confirmation after that of Marjorie's safe arrival in England, but it was not until after his liberation that he learnt of her father's death. The Liberation Letters make clear his belief that in the last months of internment the Japanese authorities completely failed to pass on letters and parcels to the internees, and that they plundered any parcels for their own use. This is confirmed in the 2nd Liberation Letter where Owen tells Marjorie that the last card he received from her was dated July 1944.

Accommodation and (Mal)nutrition

While it is reasonably certain that Owen received more news from Marjorie than she did from him, it is clear that poor communications were a major source of stress to Owen and to the other internees, a point borne out by the comments on the same topic in Hartendorp's book. Another major stress factor throughout the years of internment was the cramped and unsatisfactory conditions in which the internees lived their daily lives. In one of his Liberation Letters Owen writes:

> Do you know darling one of things I crave for most? to go into a bathroom, lock the door, and say this is mine for a whole hour!! and then to sleep in a room all by myself with my things strewn about all over the place to show that it all belongs to me! When you have lived more than cheek by jowl with hundreds of human beings you crave for solitude more than almost anything else. The first place I occupied in internment measured 6ft by 4 in the Gymnasium at Santo Tomas + there were 739 other men besides. There were 6 toilets and 4 showers – sheer misery and sometimes beastly when enteritis was prevalent. I have moved many times since those early days of /42 but I have never occupied a space more than 36 sq feet. From the Gymnasium we were moved to what is called the

Education Building – this was a lot better as were split up into groups averaging thirty in number, each group occupying separate rooms. Our actual lebensraum or living space! remained approximately the same but it was a pleasant building and we had decent toilets. Showers were constructed outside the building. I haven't had a *big* bath for years nor used any hot water: there has never been any to use, and being a tropical climate it is not necessary. Although I have grown weary of washing clothes in cold water. Lavenderas – the Spanish equivalent of wash-amahs are not paid half enough! When 800 of us were moved to Los Baňos in May 1943 most of us were housed in a Gymnasium there & still the crowded conditions prevailed. In August 1944 we were moved into large wooden, nipa roofed huts within the same camp but with no improvement in living space. One just gets bored at the sight of human beings living close-packed with them for three years & one could never get away from them. In our present situation the same condition prevails but there is all the difference in the world because we are free men well fed, & with hardly a care in the world. Strained looks & bored faces have given place to cheeriness of outlook & smiles and laughter again. It became almost a sin to be cheerful at Los Baňos during the last months. We have progressed downwards – first we occupied a University, one of the seats of higher learning in the Philippines, then we moved to an Agricultural College, and now we are living in a Prison! But still the same old arrangements {sketch of 5 beds in a row] one camp bed after another in an almost endless series as you move from building to building and when the mosquito nets are down at night the rooms look like forests of cocoons. When you have never had the use of a toilet or shower alone you will understand the craving with which this note began – and when you have slept or tried to sleep in the midst of a snoring humanity & when there was never complete quiet you begin to wonder why we are not suffering from agoraphobia which in the absence of a dictionary I believe to be 'fear of crowds'.

Owen had of course enjoyed the freedom to roam the countryside as a young boy, and probably had a study area in their accommodation in Peking. His desire for space would be fully met in the large houses and gardens which they were to occupy in Kenilworth, Daglingworth and Moreton-in-the-Marsh in the course of his 25 years of work as an

English parish priest after his return from the Philippines. As will be seen however these rambling and ill-heated properties were far from ideal from Marjorie's point of view.

Food, or the lack of it, was of course a major problem for the civilian internees in the Philippines, as it was for all those held prisoner by the Japanese during the Second World War. During the 16 months that Owen spent on the Santo Tomas campus in Manila the internal camp committee was responsible for arranging the purchase of provisions and for the cooking of meals. Reading Hartendorp's account one gains the impression that the diet was just about adequate, although inevitably monotonous. Many internees were able to supplement the camp rations with purchases from the local market that was at that time allowed to operate within the camp perimeter. In his article for the Episcopal Church Owen mentions that he received food from outside as part of the support given to him by members of the Church. The Japanese army was eventually to take responsibility for feeding the internees in Santo Tomas, and also closed down the local market in order to isolate the internees from the outside world. Given the location of the camp at Los Baňos it is probable that the army took responsibility at the outset for the supply of provisions. However it is abundantly clear, both from Owen's letters and from Hartendorp's account, that the army failed to provide adequate supplies to prevent malnutrition. Owen's estimate is that the daily allowance in the last few months of his internment came to no more than 500 calories. In the very first of the Liberation Letters he states that they had been facing slow starvation for at least the previous 5 months, and that his weight on liberation was a mere 101 pounds. The relief is obvious at the beginning of his second letter:

> I have just eaten my first piece of bread in two years and my! how delicious. All the commonplaces of normal life are now a sheer joy. To smoke again – and you will know what that means to me – to be given pieces of chocolate, butter, and jam – real coffee with milk and sugar – but it is a long list and there are more important things to write about. There is little doubt that the Santo Tomas camp committee did an excellent job in very difficult circumstances to feed the internees; little doubt also that the Japanese army signally failed to provide sufficient nourishment for the internees, in this and in other ways flouting their obligations under the

relevant international conventions. Given the number of their POWs and internees, in the Philippines and elsewhere, this would never have been an easy task, particularly after American naval victories at Coral Sea and Midway Island started to turn the tide of the war against the Japanese. The failure was however systemic, and consistent with the overall treatment of prisoners by the Japanese throughout the war years. It was Owen's misfortune to have been in the wrong place at the wrong time, having, for whatever reason, delayed his departure from Peking until it was too late for him to reach Canada before the outbreak of war between Japan and the Western Allies.

Liberation and Return

By 20th October 1944 the American army had returned to the Philippines, but it was not until late on the evening of Saturday 3rd February 1945 that they reached Manila and entered the Santo Tomas complex. It was to be a further 2 tense days before the Japanese on the premises were prevailed on to leave the camp

At dawn on Friday 23rd February American paratroopers, backed up by tanks and amphibious craft, landed at Los Baňos and evacuated the internees held there. As Owen's letters and Hartendorp's account both make clear the internees, and local guerilla groups, had believed that the Japanese had planned to shoot all of them on the approach of the American forces. The Japanese had in fact left the camp on 7th January, instructing the internees to remain within the perimeter until their liberation, but then returned on 15th January in a sour mood. The final 5½ weeks were undoubtedly the worst endured by Owen and the other internees, with totally inadequate feeding, daily deaths from malnutrition, and the constant fear of mass execution.

The American operation to liberate Los Baňos has been celebrated as one of the most daring and successful amphibious operations of the war. The operation was completed with no loss of life among the internees, and only 4 wounded. In his first letter after liberation Owen describes his rescue:

> We were freed from Los Baňos Camp yesterday morning in a miraculous way and just in the nick of time. A most dramatic exit

> by amphibian tanks across the lake into cleared territory – we left under severe fire protected on flanks by parachute troops + tank corps with a *central* drive of our captors into the hills. Oh my dear heart – I am all "churned up" – excited is too mild a term – soon we shall be able to contemplate removal from these islands but I have no news of any definite time or route. Four years of desperate longing soon to be ended & I shall be back with the three most precious persons in the world. Darlingest mine – my whole life onwards will be dedicated together with you to a more forthright service to God & the profoundest gratitude for preservation – I can say now what I could not say before – there was little hope of my seeing you again for we know now that we were destined to be shot. The relief unit arrived within 24 or 48 hours of our planned annihilation. We were facing slow starvation & had been for five months but the final despatch was beyond our imaginings. How we knew and what it is we knew I will tell you when we walk through Cranham Woods or somewhere where the sun shines on blessed English woods & fields........................
> I posses what I stand up in – shirt and shorts! we left at express speed and the camp was fired immediately on departure but I have life health – new life and love & hope with you and thank God I need nothing more. All possessions have gone, you remain and I am content oh joyfully so.
> (We are in a former Philippine prison about ten miles from Manila – there are no Japanese in this area). The American forces here are magnificent.

There was one other possession that Owen took with him when he left the camp, a small carved wooden rabbit in Netsuke style gifted to him by a fellow internee. This remained with him to the end of his life.
A letter on the following day expresses his joy at liberation and some hopes for the immediate and later future:

> It is the plan of the American Army to move practically every civilian out of the islands as soon as possible. Nothing definite is known but our guess is that in about two or three weeks we shall be on the next stage of our journey. All British civilians may be sent to Australia and I very badly want to get home the quickest way via the States. Oh! I'm so longing to get to you now that a beginning has been made – for three long weary years the longings had to be

stifled because there was no possibility of removal but the aching has increased now that the way is opening up & how impatient this always impatient person is........
I hope we shall get outfitted somewhere on the journey home and so avoid the necessity of your bringing blankets to cover me from the vulgar gaze and protect me from the coolth of England. I bet I shall find England cold after these tropical years which have for once in my life produced rather a fine mahogany colouring on the amply exposed parts of my body.
We have been handed out some late 1944 American magazines of the more 'popular' type and we are at last beginning to get out of the world of rumours & to catch up with what has been happening. I am almost a complete moron concerning the affairs of England & the world in general. Bereft of any papers or books relevant to the whole war situation one is quickly thrust into a state of mental vacuity aided materially of course by a long period of malnutrition. When I get home you will have the hardest job in the world getting me out of book shops except for meals.
No possible – or at least adequate discussion can be entered upon concerning my future but I warn you that I may ask you to consider the Philippine Islands. I seriously question any possibility of return to China for a long time even if such an invitation were received and I seriously question whether my services overseas would give me that status of seniority in any English diocese which would have been mine had I never gone overseas. This is an unpalatable truth but I believe it to be well founded. But like a damned fool I am talking in ignorance of new needs and new opportunities at home – if God grant it, a new recognition of services overseas as part of the work of the whole Church & not a cul-de-sac leading nowhere for the man who comes back. I eagerly look forward to my first interview with an English bishop or bishops!
Now I am going to another meal with even more eagerness.

Owen realised very soon that the eagerness with which he approached meals needed to be tempered with caution. In a letter dated a fortnight after the liberation he wrote:

I am continuing to keep very well & eating moderately and so trying to avoid the severe tummy troubles which have afflicted large numbers of folk whose eyes were bigger than their tummies.

> One super-meal was sufficient to warn me of the dangers of over-eating following a long period of malnutrition. The actual calorie value of our food during the latter days of internment was less than 500 – and 2100 is regarded as the necessary requirement for the maintenance of health!..........It is obvious that a sudden imposition of rich foods was fraught with danger. There were many foolish complaints during the first few days but most folk have acquired a little more mental balance since then.

The long term effects of malnutrition remained with Owen for the remainder of his life. It was to be a serious and potentially fatal stomach disorder which led to his move from Kenilworth in early 1955. The burden of a town parish and the considerable extra work involved in his post as Rural Dean proved too much for his constitution and the transfer to a quieter country parish no doubt brought with it the realisation that he would not progress further in his ecclesiastical career. The move back to another town parish in 1966 resulted in a further period of severe illness and to his eventual retirement.

While the first Americans left this holding camp on 10th March Owen's hopeful guess that he might be on his way home in no more than two or three weeks was wildly optimistic. It was not until 3rd April that he was transferred back to Santo Tomas in Manila where 5 or 6 days later, in company with many other British internees, he boarded the US troopship Admiral E W Eberle for the voyage to San Pedro (Wilmington and Los Angeles) where he disembarked on 2nd May. 3 days later he started on the long train crossing of the United States, followed by embarkation on the RMS Scythia at Halifax, and eventual disembarkation at Liverpool on 25th May and the train journey back to Gloucester to rejoin Marjorie after a separation lasting almost 52 months.

CHAPTER 8

IN ENGLAND'S GREEN AND PLEASANT LAND

A Grey Dawn Breaking

Back in England in late May 1945 Owen was, at least temporarily, without employment. He and Marjorie had returned to a country shattered by war, with food, clothes and other necessities subject to strict rationing. It was a far cry from the pleasant surroundings of the British Legation in Peking where they had spent most of their previous married life.

A return to China was out of the question. China and Japan were still at war, with Japan remaining the occupying power in Peking where there was now no British representation. Even when that war came to an untidy close after VE Day in August 1945 peace did not return to China. There were to be 4 more years of bitter civil war between the Nationalists and Communists before Mao Zedong was finally able to proclaim the foundation of the Peoples Republic on 1st October 1949. During that period of continued strife David Paton was able to return to south China and work there for 2 years, but he spoke Chinese and was able to work as a missionary with the local population. Owen, without that linguistic qualification, would not have been able to accept such a posting. As the Liberation Letters make clear he did however worry that the years spent abroad would count for nothing when it came to his prospects of advancement in the Church in England. This concern was probably justified; it is not only in the Church that years spent on secondment fall into a black hole. However, if Owen was hinting at the hope of a bishopric, it is hard to envisage him making a success of such promotion, or of enjoying it if it had been offered. Bishops need to be competent administrators, and to combine firmness with tact in their dealings with the clergy in their diocese and with all others with whom they necessarily come into contact in their daily work. While Owen handled parish business adequately it was never his preferred work, and I feel that he would have found himself out of his depth with the range of administrative work required to manage the affairs of a diocese. And again, while he had gained the respect and liking of his fellow internees in the

Philippines, he did not always display the level of tactfulness that he would have needed to make a success of a bishopric.

It was, for instance, hardly tactful to suggest in both of his first two Liberation Letters that Marjorie should seriously consider the offer made to him to return to the Philippines to take up permanent employment there, presumably with the Episcopal Church of North America. It is hardly what Marjorie would have wanted to read in the first letters that she had received from him for 4 years, and it foreshadows the future conflict between his sense of duty to his work (as he would have put it, his duty to God) and Marjorie's sense of her duty to the family, both to her mother and to the children. During her long years in Canada Marjorie had also had time to consider what her priorities in life might be, and it is reasonable to conclude that a further period of life abroad was not among them. The years of separation had taken their toll in putting a wedge between two strong and increasingly independent persons and there was no way back to the enchantment of their 7 years in China. The gulf between before and after can be clearly seen in the family photograph album. The open and relaxed faces of their China years evidence physical and emotional fulfilment. In photographs taken after the war Owen appears business-like and detached, while Marjorie's face has become closed and tense.

Money and Education

In his letters home Owen had dreamed of the opportunity to spend a quiet few months with Marjorie and the children, in a country cottage with time and space to talk, read, and tend the garden. He had also assumed that his future work would once again take him overseas. These possibilities came to nothing. Instead, very soon after his arrival back in England, he took a temporary post in the parish of Hempsted just outside Gloucester. It was not an attractive assignment. Hempsted lies in the Severn valley on the track of the Gloucester and Sharpness Canal and, despite it being summer, the house was damp. From Marjorie's point of view the compensating attraction was probably that it was an easy bus ride into central Gloucester to see her mother and brothers.

Hempsted was always a short term appointment and on 3rd October 1945 Owen took up a new permanent post as Vicar of St Nicholas parish in Kenilworth. There were to be no more foreign postings and he would remain an English parish priest until his retirement a quarter of a century later. All that remained of his post-liberation musings was the opportunity offered throughout that period to take care of the extensive gardens attached to the vicarage at Kenilworth and to the rectories at Daglingworth and Moreton-in-Marsh. There is no surviving correspondence to throw light on why Owen and Marjorie settled down to life in England, but there are several plausible reasons. As mentioned in the previous section a return to China was out of the question, and it was never likely that Marjorie would have welcomed a posting to the Philippines, a country that for her must have been emblematic of their long separation. Marjorie's mother may be assumed to have made it abundantly clear that, having just lost her husband, she did not want to lose her daughter again so soon after her bereavement. Thirteen years earlier Marjorie had thrown up her fulfilling and enjoyable work in Ambleside to return home when her mother called so that, even had an attractive foreign posting been on offer, it is likely that her strong sense of family loyalty would have led to ask that they remain in England, and not too far from Gloucester.

The overriding concern of both parents was probably however the need to ensure that John and Anthony received a proper English education. In the summer of 1945 John was approaching his tenth birthday, and his schooling up to that point had been severely disrupted by the events of the war years. At a very early age however he had set his heart on becoming an officer in the Royal Navy, and at the age of 10 he was far from possessing the educational qualifications needed to prepare him to pass the entrance examination to Dartmouth Naval College. Marjorie was prepared to make whatever sacrifices were required to ensure that her first born and favourite son had the chance to fulfil his dreams. She and Owen therefore decided that John had to attend an English public school in order to work towards the entrance examination for the Navy; and this in turn necessitated a course of study which would equip him to pass the Common Entrance examination. At the time this required, among other things, an adequate knowledge of basic Latin. This education was not available in China or the Philippines. Sending the boys as boarders to an English school would have been expensive, and there would have been no possibility of them travelling 'home' during the holidays. Owen in particular, having been separated from his family for over 4 years, would not have countenanced a renewed separation lasting for many years into the future.

Being two years younger than his brother Anthony had suffered less in educational terms from the disruptions of the war years. He was also more academically inclined, and fairness required that he should receive at least as good an education as his elder brother. If he were to apply for a university place at Oxford or Cambridge this would also require the study of Latin, in his case at least up to O Level standard. After the move to Kenilworth both boys were therefore enrolled as pupils at King's School in Coventry. This school was geared to preparing boys for the Common Entrance examination and, with 5 years of uninterrupted study, Anthony was able to sit and pass this examination without difficulty. John however, having missed 2 years out of the standard period of preparation, struggled to make the necessary progress. When it became clear that he was not on course to succeed in the examination Marjorie and Owen removed him from the school and sent him for his final year to a crammer in the south of England, where he succeeded in learning sufficient Latin to pass the examination and gain entrance to St John's School in Leatherhead. Anthony followed him 2 years later, and both completed their school life there as boarders.

A public school education, then as now, was expensive. Owen's pay as vicar of Kenilworth was £365 a year. Admittedly the vicarage was provided rent free, but this was a decidedly mixed blessing. Old vicarages and rectories, as at Kenilworth and later at Daglingworth, were large and cold. As they also acted as parish offices, with parishioners likely to drop in to see Owen at any time, Marjorie felt it essential to keep up appearances by ensuring that the downstairs part of the house was always clean and tidy. Throughout the long period from 1945 to 1970 she always required some paid help with housework and cleaning. And, although occupying their houses rent-free, parsons were required to set aside a fair proportion of their annual income towards 'dilapidations', the need to make a capital payment to the Church Commissioners on vacating the property so that the Commissioners could undertake any necessary repairs and redecoration. The word 'dilapidations' was always uttered with a sense of foreboding, as of a sword of Damocles hanging over the family finances. In brief it seems unlikely that Owen's income would have done more than cover the basic costs of food, clothes, and housekeeping. It would certainly not have been sufficient to meet the considerable expenses of a private education for the two boys. Those expenses would have comprised not only the headline item of school fees, but also the cost of uniforms, travel and sports equipment, plus some minimal pocket money to allow the boys to make some purchases of their own each term.

The China Medical Board, Owen's old employer at Peking University Medical College, had promised to pay him a full year's salary on his return to England in order to give him time and space to recover from the hardships of internment. Owen was always happiest when working, and would probably have found it difficult to kick his heels for a year, however beneficial this might have been to his physical and mental health. His decision to return to work almost immediately after his return may also reflect a joint decision that the year's salary offered by the China Medical Board should be put towards the cost of education rather than used up during an extended, and otherwise unpaid, break from employment. Additionally, Marjorie had inherited £1000 under her father's will, and this would also have made a significant contribution to the expense of educating the 2 boys.

Private education is however a long term commitment, and it seems most unlikely that the capital sums mentioned above would in themselves have been adequate to the task of funding the education of both boys throughout their lives at school. Anthony would remain in public school until the summer of 1956, so that in 1945 Owen and Marjorie knew that they were committing themselves to educational costs over at least a further 11 years. In fact those costs continued for nearly 21 years. I became a day boy at Oakley Hall preparatory school in Cirencester in September 1956, immediately after Anthony had completed his public school education at St John's School in Leatherhead, and studied there and at St John's until I left school in March 1966 to take a short break before continuing to university.

I assume that King's School in Coventry was a fee-paying establishment. It was certainly not the local school which the boys might have attended had there been no question of their preparing for the Common Entrance examination. There is no doubt that Owen and Marjorie had then to find a considerable sum to send John as a boarder to the crammer, where he lived in-house with the tutor and 3 or 4 other boys. St John's, Leatherhead, was also a fee-paying public school, although the costs were significantly reduced for the sons of clergy who made up about half of the total school population. I do not know whether there were any local public schools which John and Anthony might have attended as day boys, but possibly in any case the cost of boarding at St John's might have been less than the cost of attending a local school as day boys without any special concessions for sons of clergy. Another reason for choosing St John's may have been the feeling that the boys' education would not be disrupted if for any reason Owen was transferred to another parish.

Given the wealth of Marjorie's family it might be wondered why there were such obvious difficulties with finance. However, although Marjorie, as stated above, received an immediate legacy of £1000 under her father's will, she would not derive any further benefit from his estate until her own mother, Emily Mary, died in 1976 at the age of 94. By that time of course all three boys had long completed their education, and the additional income that she then received came too late to contribute towards those costs.

The terms of her father's will were that the business and business assets were, as one would naturally expect, left to Marjorie's brothers Arthur and John who became the new owners of the business and continued to run it until they sold out in the 1950s. As one would also naturally expect the marital home, 43 Heathville Road (known as Rosemede) was left to his widow Emily Mary. The will additionally records that Harry James Vicker had gifted the property at 31 Heathville Road to his son John in 1937 and directs his executors to ensure that the necessary conveyance is now executed in John's favour. Subject to few minor legacies, including £50 each to all his grandchildren (including John and Anthony), the residue of the estate was left on trust, with his widow Emily Mary being entitled to a life interest of all the income accruing to the trust during her lifetime.

It was Harry James's view that the business should go to his sons, the personal assets to his widow, and that his daughter should take care of her own future by marrying into another wealthy family of Gloucestershire businessmen. The fact that his final will was made in March 1944, when he knew that he was terminally ill, is clear evidence that he was not prepared to alter his fixed view of the proper way to divide the family wealth, except in so far as the £1000 specific legacy might possibly be higher than it would otherwise have been.

What is absolutely clear is that Harry James wished to entirely exclude Owen from any possible benefit under his will. The fact that he left no legacy to Owen is neutral; he left no such legacy to the wives of Arthur and John. However the terms of the trust make it clear that, on the death of Emily Mary [not until 1976 as stated above], Arthur and John would each become absolutely entitled to a 1/6th share of the assets held in the trust, while Marjorie, although benefiting from the remaining 2/3rd share, did so only as a life tenant. That 2/3rd share of the trust assets would eventually pass, on Marjorie's death, to her children, who would finally become absolutely entitled to the capital, thereby finally bringing the trust to an end.

What was all this about? The effect of the will is that neither Marjorie nor Owen would ever become entitled to any of the capital value of the estate, except for the one-off £1000 legacy to Marjorie. That Marjorie should not become entitled to a 2/3rd share of the trust assets on her mother's death, while her brothers each became fully entitled to their shares, suggests a long-standing rancorous resentment arising out of Marjorie's decision to marry Owen, and quite probably a history of misunderstanding or worse in the relationship between Harry James and his son-in-law.

I have already mentioned the question of Owen's tact in discussing whether he might have been seen as qualified for promotion to the bishopric. I do not wish to overemphasise this; after all, Owen clearly earned the respect and admiration of his parishioners in China, in the Philippines, and in all the parishes in which he worked in England after his return home. However he remained to the end very sensitive to any attack on his profession. I recall attending a meeting of the Fellowship of Vocation in Gloucester Cathedral, attended by potential candidates for ordination. Owen was there to tell the attendees what they might expect to earn as ministers. However an earlier speaker, an Anglican monk, had spoken in such a way as to suggest that the monastic vocation was superior to that of the married parish priest. Owen was immediately up in arms and, noticeably red in the face, took issue with the monk and angrily defended the role of the priest. I suspect that his father-in-law Harry James would have been equally quick to argue that the businessman played a more important role in modern society than the priest. There would have been no meeting of minds, both Harry James and Owen expressing their deep conviction of the superiority of their chosen profession and resenting the suggestion of the other that it was in some way inferior. If Owen told Harry James in plain words, as he may well have done (possibly under provocation), that the priest was doing the most important of all jobs, then it is easy to understand that Harry James would have taken this badly. Had Owen been, for instance, a lawyer or accountant with an assured income this might not have mattered. But Owen's status as an ill-paid clergyman no doubt confirmed his father-in-law in his view of Owen as a gold-digger, mainly interested in Marjorie because of her family's obvious wealth. This would have been unfair, although perhaps understandable during the long period of their engagement. It is however sad that Harry James's will, made more than 9 years after Marjorie's marriage, shows that even when faced with his own imminent death he was unable to put aside his resentment and to treat Marjorie with more fairness. With all her sense of family pride and duty there were occasions in later life when Marjorie let slip comments that betrayed her sense of personal injustice.

Clearly the £1000 legacy from her father's will was not going to be sufficient to guarantee a private education for John and Anthony over several years, without at that stage taking into consideration the possibility of future children. It does however seem likely that Marjorie's mother and her wider family shared some of her sense of injustice. Certainly her uncle George Sidney Vicker, who died in 1950, left her not only £682 as a 1/17th share of his residual estate – the same share being given to 16 other residuary legatees – but also a specific legacy of £1000. This was one of only 2 such specific legacies, the other being £500. And in 1952 Marjorie received a further £659 from the will of Lilian Irene Vicker, made up of a specific legacy of £500 and a residuary distribution of £159; this was more in line with the amount left to other beneficiaries, although Marjorie's share is once again at the higher end of the scale. My information about these legacies comes from the estate accounts kept by Marjorie among her papers. I have not seen the wills of George Sidney and Lilian Irene, so do not know if they were made after 1944, possibly altering the terms of previous wills in Marjorie's favour to compensate for the effect of her father's will.

What is also likely is that Marjorie and Owen relied to some extent on gifts from her mother, who was left with a substantial house and a comfortable income under her husband's will. Although she loved her house at Rosemede it was too large for her single occupation, and in 1952 she moved to 66 Estcourt Road, Gloucester, thereby releasing £3000 capital on the exchange. During the time of my education I gained the impression that the fees were met out of a trust arrangement. I can now see that this was not so. I may have misunderstood a comment made about the H J Vicker will trust, the one that Marjorie felt to be so unfair to her. Alternatively Marjorie may have suggested the existence of an educational trust to avoid mentioning the fact that my private education was at least partly funded by gifts from her mother. Marjorie would probably have felt entirely comfortable with money coming from an educational trust set up by her father, but to rely on subsidies from her widowed mother must have been painful to her pride as she would have seen this as equivalent to relying on charity[10].

Life and Work in Kenilworth

On 3rd October 1945 Owen was formally inducted as the new Vicar of Kenilworth in Warwickshire, a parish left vacant by the death of the previous incumbent. Owen and Marjorie moved with their 2 boys into the spacious vicarage on the old High Street, looking over the Abbey Fields and not far from the famous castle. There they were able to resume family life in a home of their own, though in circumstances very different from those that they had known in China. Clearly they resumed a full married life, since their third son Nicholas was born in June 1946. Nicholas was however born prematurely and survived for only 2 hours, being interred on 29th June in the consecrated ground of Kenilworth Cemetery. The child was named Nicholas after St Nicholas, the patron saint of Kenilworth parish church. Whether there was medical negligence on this occasion is uncertain, although Marjorie always felt that the hospital had not done all that it could to have saved Nicholas's life. If Nicholas was baptised Marjorie did not

[10] The costs of private education were also mitigated by the fact that both Anthony and I won scholarships to St John's School.

retain the certificate. Given the nature of traditional Christian belief, with the teaching that baptism was a necessary (if by no means sufficient) passport to heaven, any omission in this respect must have caused Owen and Marjorie additional pain over and above that naturally arising from the death of a child whose birth would in other circumstances have symbolised the resurrection of their marriage after their years of separation.

They were however to have a fourth child, also a boy, the author of the present work. Timothy Owen was born on 23rd September 1948 and spent the first 6½ years of his life in the vicarage at Kenilworth. I was christened Timothy after Timothy Lin, the head of the Ch'ung Tê School, where Owen and Marjorie had lived in their first period in Peking. Timothy Lin subsequently became bishop of North China when western priests left the country during the war years.

John and Anthony started their school years at St John's Leatherhead in 1949 and 1950 respectively. Attendance at this boarding school in Surrey meant that they were away from home for 8 months of each year, leaving me to grow up as almost an only child.

For Owen the move to Kenilworth represented a commitment to a new sphere of work as an English parish priest. While he had previously filled this role in Kidderminster and in Selly Oak both those posts had been temporary pending his assignment to missionary work and his return to China. In Kenilworth he was in for the long haul of running a parish, with the all the associated work of maintaining effective personal relationships with his parishioners ensuring that any disagreements were nipped in the bud. He undertook this work with his customary full commitment and enthusiasm, and the life of the family inevitably revolved around his routines. Parish work in Kenilworth would have been very different to his earlier work in China and the Philippines, but Owen did not regret the change or wish to return to the missionary field. He became known as the cycling vicar, featured as such in a local newspaper article, and returned to the cricket field in the summer months. The vicarage also possessed a large garden, including a substantial vegetable patch, and Owen spent much time there, finding in his old love of gardening a fulfilling relaxation from the stresses of running a busy parish. His work must have impressed the Bishop, since in November 1948 he was appointed

Rural Dean of Kenilworth with his responsibility covering the parishes of Allesley, Berkswell, Eastern Green, Finham, Great & Little Packington, Kenilworth (both parishes), Leek Wootton, Meriden, Stoneleigh (home of the Royal Agricultural Show) and Westwood with Fletchamstead. Those whose understanding of the duties of a Dean is based on a reading of Trollope's Barchester novels may be surprised by the extent of the duties comprised in the formal instructions given to Owen on his appointment:

1. The Rural Dean is to give information to the Bishop of all matters concerning the Clerty, and the institutions and affairs of the Parishes within his Rural Deanery, which he may deem it necessary or useful that the Ordinary should know, and he is to give information to the Archdeacon of all matters concerning Churchwardens and other officers of the Church.
2. He is to visit the several Parishes in his Deanery when he is requested to do so by the Bishop, not less than once in three years (except when the Bishop or Archdeacon visits), and make a return to the Archdeacon on a form supplied to him for that purpose, for the information of the Bishop, in regard to all the Articles of Enquiry specified in the return paper. The return is to be based on his own observations, *and not on information supplied by others*.
3. He is to examine and correct the inventory of Church goods, and if such inventory does not exist to see that one is carefully made by the Incumbent and Churchwardens. He is to see that ancient brasses and other memorials are properly preserved. He is also to see that the buildings are adequately insured.
4. He is to give information to the Bishop and Archdeacon of the avoidance of any benefice within his Deanery, in order that due enquiry may be made into the state of the vacant benefice, and sequestration, if necessary, issued out of the Ecclesiastical Court.
5. He will be present at the public Institution of any Incumbent in his Deanery, and, in the absence of the Archdeacon, induct him on receiving the Archdeacon's Mandate.

6. He must assist the Bishop is seeing that Assistant Curates are duly licensed, and that no Clergyman, not already licensed in the Diocese, is permitted to officiate for more than one Sunday without the Bishop's sanction.
7. He must be ready to advise and assist the Churchwardens within his Deanery in framing their presentments of all such things as are amiss within their respective Parishes, and are by law presentable.
8. He must be ready to assist the Parochial Church Council in performance of their duties.
9. It is his duty to see that Parochial Church Meetings are held in due time for the election of Parochial representatives, and to summon them, when elected, to the Ruridecanal Conference, so that elections to the Convention be made.
10. It is his duty to see that no unlicensed lay person perform duty in a consecrated building except by special permission of the Bishop, and that no licensed person performs other duties than those specified in the licence, or in any other manner than that permitted by the regulations for Lay Readers, except by special permission of the Bishop.
11. It is further his duty to assemble for other purposes as the Bishop shall direct, both the Chapter of the Clergy, and the Ruridecanal Conference of the Clerical and Lay Representatives. Wherever it is practicable, four Meetings should be held in each year, two at least of which should be a Meeting of the Conference.
12. He is to perform such other duties as may from time to time be entrusted to him by the Bishop.

The final clause requiring performance of 'anything else your boss requires' will no doubt be easily recognised by all those who have negotiated performance agreements with their employers.

Owen would have taken these responsibilities seriously, frequently cycling to the outlying parishes to ensure that their incumbents and churchwardens were complying with their obligations under Church law and regulations. One hopes that he was not faced with the unpleasant duty of making any adverse reports to the Bishop on matters covered by clauses 1 and 2 of the instructions. I have however reproduced the document in full partly to demonstrate the wide range of responsibilities involved in running a parish within the Church of England, and the level of knowledge of legal technicalities expected of the Clergy. For instance the 'Ordinary' mentioned in clause 1 is defined in Chambers Dictionary as 'a judge of ecclesiastical or other causes who acts in his own right, as a bishop or his deputy'.

Marjorie's Life at Kenilworth – The Broken Bowl

While Owen was able to find new fulfilment in his parish work and in his garden, Marjorie found it much harder to adjust to her new life. Her previous experience of married life in England had been in the cramped conditions of the flat in Selly Oak in the year between their two spells in China. The vicarage at Kenilworth was, by contrast, spacious, but a large house without central heating brought its own problems, particularly during the notoriously harsh winter of 1947 when the property was undergoing substantial reconstruction. Now that the vicarage was the parish office, where Owen received his visitors, Marjorie had to work hard, with limited domestic assistance, to ensure that at least the downstairs areas were maintained at a level of cleanliness and tidiness appropriate to a public area; visitors after all could arrive at any time, even if most no doubt came by prior appointment. Throughout the years from 1945 to 1951 severe wartime rationing restrictions remained in force, and this added considerably to the pressures of feeding a growing family on a very limited budget. If I am right in my earlier suggestion that Owen and Marjorie were dependent, at least to some extent, on gifts from Marjorie's mother towards the education of the 2 older boys, then Marjorie would have been bitterly conscious of this fact in ensuring that the family incurred no other expenses that might have been seen as in any way extravagant.

With a new child and a large house to keep in order Marjorie must have looked back with longing to the domestic help that she had enjoyed in China, the amah to take care of the children, the cook and probably one or more other servants. With this level of assistance she had been able to recreate something of her Ambleside life in the easy comradeship of a group with similar intellectual and general interests, and to enjoy to the full the social life of the Legation Quarter. In talking of her life Marjorie always came back to Ambleside and China as her golden periods; it is clear that Kenilworth did not come close.

Nevertheless Kenilworth was a town parish where Marjorie was able to walk to the shops and to make some good friends with whom she would remain in touch throughout her later life.

What domestic help she had was a few hours each week from a local woman who came in to assist with the housework and cleaning. It is likely that Marjorie felt it necessary to exercise fairly close supervision, as she did not delegate easily. And when the cleaner dropped and broke a valuable 17th century Chinese bowl given as a wedding present this must have symbolised for Marjorie the fracturing of her hopes for a fulfilling life.

Holidays, while giving Owen a necessary and welcome respite from parish duties, probably provided little respite for Marjorie. 1949 saw a trip to Torquay. I have no memory or record of holidays taken in the following 2 years, but in 1952 the family made the first of two trips to Rye Harbour. They rented, or were given the use of, one of the bungalows situated in middle of the marshes behind the beach, a mile's walk from the nearest shop. The bungalows are still there, and now sell for high prices, but in the early 1950s they were fairly basic, probably with no mains electricity or gas. Without a car Owen could not drive his family there and take them on journeys around the adjoining country. However Sir John Savage, a senior executive in the Land Rover company and one of the churchwardens in |Kenilworth, arranged for the family to be driven there and back in a Land Rover. The family returned there in the following year, but no holiday was possible in 1954 since Owen became seriously ill with a stomach complaint and spent some weeks in bed, where he employed part of his time in reorganising his stamp collection. His doctor advised him that the work of a busy town parish, added to his duties as Rural Dean, was too much for him and that he would likely die within a year if he did not move to a quieter post. In February 1955 therefore Owen and Marjorie moved themselves and their family to Daglingworth, a small village outside Cirencester, where they were to spend the next eleven and a half years of their married life.

Daglingworth

Daglingworth was a small village with a population rather under 150. It then had 2 small shops, one acting as the post office, and a community hall which was burnt down and rebuilt during the period that Owen and Marjorie lived in the parish. There was no pub, although the village did field a cricket team in the summer on the field adjoining the glebe. The full title of Owen's new role was Rector of Daglingworth and the Duntisbournes, and he therefore had responsibility not only for the church in Daglingworth itself, but also for the tiny Saxon church at Duntisbourne Rous and the somewhat larger church at Duntisbourne Abbots at the head of the valley. This was Cotswold country, with several farms, a manor house and squire in Daglingworth, and the wealthy Birchall family in Duntisbourne Abbots.

Owen's initial problem was transport. He acquired a bicycle with an auxiliary motor to help him negotiate the hills on the 3 mile road leading from one end of the valley to the other, but soon some parishioners had got together to provide him with a car, an original Ford Popular (ROF 737) with 3 gears and no synchromesh between first and second gear. He was now able to choose between the narrow and twisting valley road and the main A417 Ermine Street which, appropriately for a Roman road, ran in a straight line parallel to the valley. When I moved from the village school and, at the age of 8, started my preparatory school studies in Cirencester in the autumn of 1956 Owen was able to ferry me back and forth each morning and evening until I started boarding there in 1959 or 1960.

With three churches to look after Sunday was inevitably a busy day. Owen would officiate at three or four services, and would probably preach his sermon at least twice. As far as I am aware Owen never preached any sermon that he had not written himself and, apart from preaching the same sermon in 2 or 3 different churches on the same Sunday, never repeated his previous sermons. He would sit down in his study each Friday morning and laboriously type his text on an old Underwood typewriter. When he died he left behind him a large number of boxes containing all his sermons. Marjorie kept them, saying that she wished to read them again. Whether she did so I do not know, but in any event she did not keep them.

Owen was a quiet middle of the road Anglican. He was happy with the 1662 and 1928 Book of Common Prayer, dressed normally in a cassock when he was out of the house and wore a surplice and stole in church. He was in no way attracted to the elaborate ritual and incense of the Anglo-Catholic tradition, and also had no leanings towards Evangelical fundamentalism. His time in internment had taught him to work with ministers from other denominations, and he avoided, so far as possible, all those doctrinal disputes that tended to exaggerate the differences between different groups of Christians. In his later life he was to play a role within the Gloucester diocese in discussions on a potential merger between the Anglican and Methodist churches. While he would probably not have felt comfortable in holding similar discussions with the representatives of the Roman Catholic Church he did not waste his energy in criticising the beliefs and practices of that organisation. As he had said in one of his Liberation Letters his time in camp had made him acutely aware that divisions between the different denominations were not understood even by otherwise sympathetic outsiders, so that, while remaining himself comfortable with the Anglican community, he was able to regard other denominations as seeking God in their own way.

Although parish work was probably lighter at Daglingworth than at Kenilworth, with the added factor that Owen was no longer acting as Rural Dean for a group of parishes, the house was somewhat larger and the garden very much larger. This gave Owen ample scope to work outside, growing vegetables in a patch at least double the size of a standard allotment, together with a large cage for soft fruit and a thriving orchard. The vegetables and fruit made an important contribution to the family housekeeping, with apples being stored over the winter in one of the spacious cellars under the house. Maintenance of the garden, including the mowing of 2 large lawns, was hard work but gave Owen plenty of exercise in the open air doing something that he had always enjoyed.

Marjorie's lot was much less happy. She had to look after another large and unheated rectory more or less by herself, though with some help from Kate Green, a woman from the village who came in once a week to provide assistance and some welcome companionship. Marjorie however found herself isolated in a small country village where the 2 small shops had limited stocks and high prices. She had never learned to drive and trips into the local town of Cirencester required her to take the infrequent bus service and do what shopping she could carry with her one good arm. Away from Kenilworth she also lost the opportunity for meeting like-minded friends. While she felt reasonably at home with the wife of the local squire and with a teacher who set up a small private school in the village there was no day to day contact. The same held true of her acquaintance with the families living at the other end of the valley in Duntisbourne Abbots where, in the absence of any bus service, she relied entirely on Owen being able to drive her there in the car. As a result social meetings took place rather rarely, mainly as a result of more or less formal invitations to coffee or a very occasional meal. It did not help Marjorie that she was never able to socialise easily with those with whom she shared no intellectual interests, and she also disapproved of the few short-lived friendships that I made with village boys whom she regarded as common. Partly through choice therefore, but much more through force of circumstance, she felt trapped in a life which offered her no chance of escape and self-fulfilment. While Owen had his work and his garden to keep him fully occupied, and the boys went off happily to boarding school to enjoy a comradeship not on offer in the village, Marjorie was left to look after a rambling house and continue the struggle to make ends meet on a severely limited budget. It is perhaps not surprising therefore, as she confessed to me towards the end of the years in Daglingworth, that she had contemplated divorce, being restrained only by her sense of duty to Owen in his role as a priest and knowing how devastating a separation would be for his position in the community. That she, a committed member of the Mothers' Union, should have gone so far as to consider the possibility suggests that, over and above the problems that I have outlined above, the relationship between Owen and herself had gone cold. It was very obvious to me as a young boy that any expression of emotion was off limits; one of Marjorie's most frequent rebukes to me being "don't speak to me in that tone of voice".

The eldest son John, with some additional coaching, had succeeded in passing the entrance examination for Dartmouth Royal Naval College. There was then a crisis when he failed an eyesight test and diagnosed by the naval doctor with Menière's disease which, if correct, would have ruled out any career as an officer on board ship. Marjorie took matters in hand over several months, paying for him to see a private consultant who disagreed with the diagnosis and finally succeeded in persuading the Navy that John had been suffering from flu at the time of the original test. All ended happily with John being allowed to go ahead and become a fully-fledged naval officer. This inevitably involved much foreign travel, and John fully lived up to his character as the blue-eyed boy by writing immensely long letters home every week and, after various flirtations, marrying Margaret Anne Eggins, the daughter and only child of a very respectable Devon farmer. During their years together in Australia, where their only son Michael was born, and then in Singapore Anne took over much of the weekly letter writing, managing to outdo even John in the length of many of these epistles.

Anthony meanwhile had fulfilled his academic promise at St John's School in Leatherhead, and had also been given his first interest in mountaineering by his housemaster Tom Peacocke, a climber who had been ruled out of the 1953 Everest expedition solely on account of his age. Anthony gained entrance to University College, Oxford, where he pursued the study of classics and in due course took his degree and entered the teaching profession. His first job was at Oakley Hall school in Cirencester where he had to teach to Latin and Greek to a class including his young brother, the present author. He then became engaged to and married Felicity (Flicky) Coombs, an assistant nurse working at the school, but seriously blotted his family reputation when their first daughter Nicola was born just over 7 months after the wedding. Owen and Marjorie were totally shattered by this, regarding premarital sex as a mortal sin. By this time Anthony and Flicky were living at a preparatory school in Sussex. Owen was all for driving straight down to Sussex and lecturing them, but was dissuaded by Marjorie. I got the lecture instead, from Marjorie. What Owen and Marjorie regarded as a mortal sin, Flicky's parents regarded as a social *faux pas*, and Flicky herself, when I mentioned things to her, dismissed it as 'a mistake with contraceptives'. This was in 1963, at the start of the sexual revolution of that decade, and the different reactions to Nicola's birth mirror the conflicts unleashed by that change in *mores*. Owen should perhaps have recollected that his eldest brother had also been born rather soon after his parents' marriage and have reflected that his criticism of Anthony and Flicky implied similar criticism of his own beloved mother.

Daglingworth Holidays

No doubt in main part because of the costs of private education Owen and Marjorie's budget remained very tight during the Daglingworth years. The housekeeping budget was notably restricted, with limited variety in the food on the table. 'Best end of neck' was a treat; 'scrag end' more normal. Another reason for the emphasis on cheap and plain food was probably the continuing worry that Owen, after his years in camp, was unduly to cope with richer food. Marjorie did however make full use of the opportunities provided by the orchard and fruit cage to prepare excellent desserts.

I have no recollection of the holidays, if any, taken in 1955 and 1956. In one of those years, probably in 1955, Owen went by himself on a retreat to Iona. This helped him to recover from his illness and to focus his energies for the task ahead. In 1957 He agreed to swap duties for a fortnight with a priest running a parish in a small village adjoining the Queen's estate at Sandringham. This was not a success, and the experiment was never repeated. Marjorie had very high standards of cleanliness in her own house, even higher standards in other properties. The whole family had therefore to tread on eggshells to ensure that the borrowed house was in spick and span condition when we left it. On our return home Marjorie was distressed to find that the visiting children had played with a model land rover given to her by Sir John Savage in the early years of its production. What might have been quite a valuable heirloom had been sorely knocked around.

For 2 or 3 years after that the family holidayed in a cliffside chalet at Branscombe in Devon – the chalets have since succumbed to subsidence of the whole cliff. And after that they rented for another 2 or 3 years a small cottage on the edge of the cliffs at Penycwm in Pembrokeshire, an idyllic situation except for its position directly under the flight path for RAF Brawdy and about 400 yards from the end of the runway. The Pembrokeshire cottage had no electricity, apart from that generated by a small wind turbine in the garden, and no mains water; the water had to be fetched in a bucket from the local spring and then boiled on a cooker working on calor gas. There was also no sanitation. On the final day of each holiday Owen would bury the contents of the Elsan toilet in a new hole in the garden, and

Marjorie would clear the family out of the house to spend most of the day in a carrying out a full spring-clean. Obviously these holidays were all self-catering, so that Marjorie still had to ensure that the family was fed, preparing a cooked breakfast and cooking vegetables to accompany slices from the large cold ham prepared at home before our departure.

There was little change in these arrangements when Owen and Marjorie rented a small caravan sitting all by itself in a field in Snowdonia. Again there was neither electricity or running water, and Owen and the boys (then Anthony and myself) would wash in the local stream from which we also fetched the water. It is a matter of no small surprise that this small and primitive caravan still sat in the same field nearly half a century later and may indeed still be there.

In 1961 however the parishioners offered Owen and Marjorie the unexpected chance to attend the Passion Play in Oberammegau, followed by a few days in the Austrian Tyrol. And in 1966, probably because it was already known that Owen would be moving to another parish, the same parishioners offered them a trip to Israel and Jordan where they were able to visit the places which were for them so inextricably linked with the biblical narrative. Over the years the generosity of the parishioners had also extended to regular supplies of logs for the fires, the logs being delivered from a farm trailer directly into the cellar through an external hatch, and more occasional gifts of pheasants and other game.

Moreton-in-Marsh

In 1966, when Owen was approaching his 65th birthday and might have expected to be left to continue his work quietly in Daglingworth for a few more years, the Bishop of Gloucester asked if he would consider taking on the small town parish of Moreton-in-Marsh. As a Church of England priest Owen could have told the Bishop that he preferred to stay in his existing parish, but as always his sense of duty and of obedience led him, much against his personal inclination, to accept the invitation. The parish had suffered its own problems, with differences between the parishioners and between the parishioners and the previous incumbent. Owen was expected to sort these out, in addition to handling the normal work of officiating at the main church in Moreton-in-Marsh and the smaller church in the outlying village of Batsford. The job came with another large house and garden. From Marjorie's point of view there was perhaps some compensation in that she was once again within walking distance of a reasonable range of shops.

At about the time of the move it had become apparent that Marjorie's mother was no longer able to cope on her own in her house in Gloucester, and Marjorie and Owen offered to accommodate her in an upstairs room with an adjoining bathroom. She was to live with the family for 3 or 4 years, suffering increasingly from mobility problems and putting an added strain on Marjorie as effectively her carer. After a live of relying on servants she assumed that Marjorie would always be at her beck and call.

In previous chapters I have mentioned Owen's involvement in the aftermath of the murder of Pamela Werner in Peking, and his involvement with the internees executed by the Japanese in the camp in Manila. He might reasonably have expected not to have to experience any similar problems in his new parish. However the young and popular local GP, married with a charming wife and two fine children, drove out one day with his mistress and, having made an unsuccessful attempt to persuade her to live with him, shot her and then turned the gun on himself. It was of course Owen who had to sit with the widow and start the process of helping her to face up to the tragedy and to cope with the anguish of her children.

Perhaps in partial compensation for the unwelcome move of parish the Bishop, in early 1969, offered Owen the post of Honorary Canon of Gloucester Cathedral, a role which involved some attendance at the Cathedral and some work in showing visitors around. More importantly it was the Bishop's way of thanking Owen for the work that he had carried in the diocese over many years. Owen received over 30 letters of congratulation, mainly from his fellow clerics. Several mentioned specifically the work that he had done since his return from the Philippines to promote the missionary work of the Church. He had consistently played a leading role in diocesan efforts in this field, and had taken a particular interest in the missionary work in Car Nicobar and the Andaman Islands, welcoming representatives from that diocese when they came to England, though never himself being in a position to visit this remote area – an area which suffered massive damage long after Owen's death in the 2004 tsunami. Perhaps however the most touching letter that Owen received came from a forgotten acquaintance of his youth, a man who had worked in the local post office at Bushley when Owen was growing up in Queenhill and who had followed Owen's career with interest ever since, even cycling over from Birmingham to Kenilworth on a few occasions to hear his sermons at the evening service.

The proper title of Owen's parish was Batsford with Moreton-in-Marsh, and it was the small church and hamlet at Batsford that provided him with the incentive to start work on the ecclesiastical history of that community, centred around the large house and park occupied by Lord Dulverton of the Wills tobacco family. In his retirement he was able to complete this study, although, as far as I am aware, it was never published. Lord Dulverton offered Owen and Marjorie the use of their 'holiday cottage' for one holiday. This turned out to be another spacious mansion on the shores of Loch Eil on the road to Mallaig, and they were able to combine a few days there with a visit to their son John, with his wife Anne and child Michael, in the much smaller cottage that they then inhabited near Loch Long (John was at this time working on the Faslane submarine base).

Parish work continued to be onerous, and in 1969 or early 1970 Owen once again suffered from serious stomach problems. It was probably as a result of this that he was permitted to retire in October 1970, a year before he reached 70, the usual retirement age for clergymen in the Anglican church.

Winchcombe

On their retirement Owen and Marjorie bought a small new terraced house in Winchcombe. With a single living room, a kitchen with a dining area, and 3 modest upstairs bedrooms, it was a far cry from the large rectory houses that they inhabited for the preceding 25 years. However it came with a reasonably sized garden plot, albeit on quite a steep slope, and Owen was able for some time to enjoy himself in shaping yet another garden. Apart from working on his history of Batsford, and contributing his time to discussions between the Anglicans and Methodists on possible unification, he also decided to revisit his study of the history of English literature, on which he had lectured during his internment. He bought the first volume of the Pelican history of English Literature, but it was not too long before it became clear that he would not complete this study. He maintained his interest in sport, a special treat being a visit with a friend to Cardiff Arms Park to see one of the Welsh international matches.

In 1974 the Bishop wrote to him, asking him for his views on whether clergy who had retired from parish duties should continue to occupy stalls in the cathedral as honorary canons. Owen understood this, as it was intended to be understood, as a request that he should resign his stall, and did so. He then became a Canon Emeritus, allowed to retain his title but no longer having the right to give the occasional sermon in the cathedral. He did however feel hurt by the Bishop's letter, particularly, I think, by the way in which it was worded. The Bishop had clearly come to a decision on the way forward, and Owen felt that he was being given no choice but to go along with the fiction that he was being given a choice in the matter.

Three or four years after his retirement Owen suffered his first heart attack. He was advised by his doctor to give up smoking, which he managed, but his health continued to deteriorate. When he started getting confused it became time for him to sell his car and cease driving – a blessing in disguise for other road users as he had always seemed to believe in his divine right of way on roundabouts. With Alzheimer's disease however the road from now on was steadily downhill, with once familiar things becoming strange and threatening – for instance he could no longer tune in with eager anticipation to the broadcast of a rugby international on the television, now pleading for it to be turned off as he could not understand why those people were fighting. He was no longer able to hold a conversation, but remained aware enough to make frequent apologies for his failure in this respect. Finally, on 20th December 1978 he suffered his third and final heart attack, with the burial service taking place a week later in Daglingworth Church where his ashes were interred in a grave space overlooking the old Rectory where he and Marjorie had spent 11 years of their life.

After Owen's death Marjorie lived at their retirement property in Winchcombe for a further 4½ years. It was in many ways convenient for her. She could walk to the shops in the village, and the house itself was modern and modestly-sized, making the job of housework much easier. It was also on a bus route, which meant that she could get easily into Cheltenham with its much greater range of shops. While her mother was still alive, and living in a retirement home in Gloucester, Marjorie had been able to take buses from Winchcombe via Cheltenham to Gloucester and spend time with her. The house therefore met her stated requirement that, if you have one foot in the grave, it is best to have the other foot on a bus stop.

In the autumn of 1982 however Marjorie was knocked over by a car reversing in one of the local car parks, the car ironically being driven by the manager of an old people's home. In her fall she broke her hip and the wrist of her good arm. Not being able to put any weight on either hand she was unable to practise walking on her new hip for some time and developed severe arthritis. Although she managed to return home she was not now able to use the stairs, and had therefore to sleep downstairs with no access to the bathroom – fortunately the house had a downstairs toilet, but she was no longer able to do more than wash herself in the basin. It was therefore agreed that she would sell the house and move to Guildford to live with the present author and his wife, who also put their house on the market and looked for a bungalow with a workable granny flat. By moving to Guildford she also moved much closer to her eldest son John and his wife Anne, who had for many years lived just outside Portsmouth and who were therefore now within easy visiting distance. Marjorie lived in Guildford for the next 3 years, but her increasingly impaired mobility meant that she came to require professional help with washing and dressing. When in 1986 I was offered a post in Swansea, Marjorie made it clear that she did not wish to move there and opted for a retirement home a few miles from John and Anne. This was probably her best choice, although she was never very happy there, keeping largely to her room and declining to mix with the other residents. In early 1987 she developed severe stomach problems, but declined to talk to the doctor whom she mistrusted. Eventually she went into hospital for an operation to bypass a massive stomach ulcer, but survived the operation for only a few weeks before suffering a major stroke and dying on 13th December 1987. Her ashes were interred in the graveyard of Daglingworth Church, where she shares Owen's burial plot.

Printed in Great Britain
by Amazon

48180952R00067